When It's Twilight Time

30 Worship Services
For Retirement Settings

Clement E. Lewis

CSS Publishing Company, Inc.
Lima, Ohio

WHEN IT'S TWILIGHT TIME

Scripture quotes are from:
The *New Revised Standard Version of the Bible,* copyrighted 1989 by the Division of Christian Education of the National Council of the Churches of Christ in the USA. Used by permission.

The *Revised Standard Version of the Bible,* copyrighted 1946, 1952, (c), 1971, 1973, by the Division of Christian Education of the National Council of the Churches of Christ in the USA. Used by permission.

The *King James Version of the Bible,* in the public domain.

The *Holy Bible, New International Version, copyright (c) 1973, 1978, 1984 International Bible Society. Used by permission of Zondervan Bible Publishers. All rights reserved.*

The *Living Bible* (c) 1971. Used by permission of Tyndale House Publishers, Inc., Wheaton, IL 60189. All rights reserved.

Library of Congress Cataloging-in-Publication Data

Lewis, Clement E., 1918-
    When it's twilight time : 30 worship services for health care centers, retirement homes, and other special life settings / Clement E. Lewis.
        p.   cm.
    ISBN 1-55673-837-4
    1. Worship programs. 2. Church work with the aged. 3. Aged—Prayer-books and devotions—English. I. Title.
BV199.A64L48   1994
264'.0087—dc20   93-42515
                                                                                CIP

ISBN 1-55673-837-4   PRINTED IN U.S.A.

*This book is dedicated to the
residents, staff and volunteers
of
Morningside Ministries
at
The Manor, The Meadows, and Chandler Center
San Antonio, Texas,
and to the author's wife
Dorothy Miller Lewis.*

Contents

Special Occasion Themes

Introduction

It is not unusual to hear people refer to "the twilight years," as they think of retirement, cessation of the rush of life's activities, and the opportunity to share reflective moments, relaxation and the joy of being quietly thankful for meaningful experiences.

Twilight is a most pleasant time of the day and should be eagerly anticipated. My wife, Dorothy, and I often sit on the patio, enjoying the gentle breeze and the slowly dissipating light, minus the glare and heat of the sun. As lights come on in homes, stars begin to peek through the dimming sky and birds settle into their night-time roosts, it is good to realize how gently and lovingly God promises rest and peace. It is a wonderful time for sharing meaningful events and looking forward to blessings yet to come.

In spite of physical deficiencies that accompany the human ripening processes and the accumulation of calendar years, we can enjoy the gradual spin-down of life's pace and the beauty of softness that comes when it's twilight time if we continue to be creative of mind, heart, faith and fellowship. In it we recognize that darkness and rest will come as natural relief from our labors.

The light that remains after the sun sinks past the western border is caused by rays of the sun which are bent, or refracted, by the earth's atmosphere, so that they still reach the earth and the light lasts until the sun is about 18 degrees below the horizon. If we travel north or south, we find that the sun's path across the earth varies, causing the length of twilight to vary. Our twilight years may also vary, depending on where we are in our journey of life. Actually, twilight years seem to be increasing for many who are no longer limited by the idea of the three score and 10 average and many are living well beyond a century, making the twilight experience even longer.

There is a song, known by two different titles, that speaks of the twilight, its beauty and its precious moments shared by those we love. One of the titles is "Just A Song at Twilight" and the other is "Love's Old Sweet Song" with lyrics by G. Clifton Bingham and music by J. L. Molloy. The words are from a 19th century writer, and so far as I could learn, it is his only published work. Here is the refrain, perhaps you also know the tune.

Just a song at twilight, when the lights are low,
And the flick'ring shadows softly come and go;
Tho' the heart be weary, sad the day and long,
Still to us at twilight, comes love's old song,
comes love's old sweet song.

Being among the "twilighters" after 42 years in local church pastoral ministry and more than a decade serving as chaplain in a retirement home and nursing ministry, and remembering that song, I suggest that this book should bear the title, *When It's Twilight Time.* Thank you for sharing it with everyone you can.

Clement E. Lewis

Some Uses For This Book

A helpful resource for:
- Nursing homes, retirement centers, hospitals, chaplains' and ministers' resource shelves, shut-ins at home.
- Women's, men's, youth groups, Sunday school classes.
- Public, institutional and private libraries.
- Volunteers, visitors, and families to use as devotional moments when going to see patients or residents.
- Pastors and lay speakers will find in this book a source for illustrations and aids to worship.
- Personal gifts for the elderly and home-bound folks.

1
The Miracle Of Life

Instrumental Meditation

Introductory Moments

Hymn: "Take My Life And Let It Be"

Prayer Of Invocation:
Our Father, we come into your holy presence, with thanksgiving that you have given us life, and the capacity to enjoy it and to live it meaningfully. Continue to nurture our souls, we pray, that we may grow in grace and knowledge, and do your will more perfectly. Grant that we may ever remember that we were made in your image, and should do all possible to retain its sacred design. These things we pray in the name of Jesus Christ your Son our Lord. Amen.

Scripture: Psalm 139:13-15 (NRSV)
It was you who formed my inward parts;
you knit me together in my mother's womb.
I praise you, for I am fearfully and wonderfully made.
Wonderful are your works; that I know very well.
My frame was not hidden from you, when I was being made
in secret, intricately woven in the depths of the earth.

Hymn: "Master, Speak! Thy Servant Heareth"

Sermon: "The Miracle Of Life"

One of the most beautiful descriptions of the beginning and awareness of life is found in these words from the 139th Psalm. This is poetry in its most intimate expression, and it applies to each of us.

The story of creation as found in Genesis is inspiring and basic to the understanding of the initiation of life into the world. It is especially meaningful when we read: "Then the Lord God formed man from the dust of the ground, and breathed into his nostrils the breath of life; and the man became a living being." (Genesis 2:7) But here in the 139th Psalm natural procreation is described and praised, as it should be. Both passages proclaim that life is the natural gift of God, by means of developmental process and the gift of human consciousness.

The psalmist had very little medical knowledge by which to describe the conception and pregnancy process, but he possessed something more important — a true religious appreciation for the miracle of life. He knew nothing of genetics, the sciences of obstetrics, gynecology, or pediatrics — but he knew who had the power to cause life, and he was glad! He had no X-ray or sonar by which to observe the inner growth process, but he knew that God caused a growth miracle to take place within his mother's womb, and he believed that only God could bring that to happen, then to empower him to become a living, breathing human being, with common identity with others like himself.

He also believed that God had a purpose for each life, and that every life was precious to him. The Psalm, in its entirety, deals with the omnipresence and the omniscience of God in relation to each one of us. God is everywhere, and he is all-knowing, and the wonder of it is that he cares about the well-being and the nurture of each life, and of all lives together. God wants the best for all of us, and for each one of us, yet he limits himself. He created us in his image, but he endowed us with the gift of free-will — the ability to make choices on our own, to be creative and upright by self-determination.

12

God ordains that life should be good, and that goodness and righteousness should be our way of life, yet the determination is up to each one of us.

The consciousness of the greatness of the miracle of life causes the psalmist to say:

"How precious to me are thy thoughts, O God!
How vast the sum of them!
If I would count them, they are more than the
sand." (Psalm 139:17-18 — RSV)

The psalmist recognized that we must be aware of the purpose of life, as well as its wonder. Leo Rosten put the idea into effective words. He said, "The purpose of life is not to be happy — but to matter, to be productive, to be useful, to have it make some difference that you lived at all."

Socrates said, "The end of life is to be like God, and the soul following God will be like him." That is what God wills for each of us.

Albert Schweitzer has told us: "By having reverence for life, we enter into a spiritual relation with the world."

This verse by Ella Wheeler Wicox says it well:

"Our lives are songs; God writes the words
And we set them to music at pleasure;
And the song grows glad, or sweet or sad,
As we choose to fashion the measure."

A Prayer:

O God our Father, thank you for giving us the miracle of life, by which to enjoy the glories of creation, the joy of human and spiritual fellowship, and the wonders of your love. We marvel at the birth of a child, and our hearts leap with joy that you entrust us human beings with the care of those born so helpless that they need prenatal and societal care for development and the bonds of love and understanding. We rejoice that life ripens, years lengthen, and wisdom and grace prosper when we reverence life. Grant that we may continually rejoice in the knowledge that we are made in your image, and that no matter how strong or weak we feel ourselves to be, we continually have the blessing and comfort of your eternal presence. Amen.

The Lord's Prayer *(Prayed by everyone)*

The Parting Hymn: Fourth stanza of "Take My Life And Let It Be"

Take my will and, make it Thine,
It shall be no longer mine;
Take my heart it is Thine own,
It shall be thy royal throne.

Refrain:
Lord I give my life to Thee,
Thine for evermore to be;
Lord I give my life to Thee,
Thine for evermore to be. Amen.

The Mizpah Benediction: *(May be said in unison)*
The Lord watch between you and me, when we are absent one from another. Amen.

2
The Virtue Of Self-Management

Instrumental Meditation

Words Of Preparation from Isaiah 55:6-7
Seek the Lord while he may be found,
call upon him while he is near,
let the wicked forsake his way,
and the unrighteous their thoughts;
let them return to the Lord, that he may have mercy on them,
And to our God, for he will abundantly pardon.

A Prayer Of Preparation: *(May be offered in unison)*
　　Almighty God, unto whom all hearts are open, all desires known, and from whom no secrets are hid: Cleanse the thoughts of our hearts by the inspiration of your Holy Spirit, that we may perfectly love you, and worthily magnify your holy name; through Jesus Christ our Lord. Amen.

Hymn: "A Charge To Keep I Have"

Scripture: Proverbs 3:5-6; 11-12; 25:28
Trust in the Lord with all your heart and lean not on your
　　own understanding;
in all your ways acknowledge him, and he will make your paths
　　straight.

15

My son, do not despise the Lord's discipline and do not resent
his rebuke
because the Lord disciplines those he loves, as a father the son
delights in.

Like a city breached, without walls, is one who lacks self-
control.

Sermon: "The Virtue Of Self-Management"

When we fail to develop the virtue of self-management,
we end up cursing ourselves with a lack of clear thinking, failure
to reason properly, and making inappropriate decisions. Good
self-management requires patience, thoroughness, and perseverance.

There are three sentences that people say which demonstrate the virtue of self-management has not been cultivated.
They are: "I can't help myself." "I don't care." "I don't feel
responsible; let someone else do it." All of these are referred
to as cop-outs by those who accomplish things that need doing.

"I can't help myself," is a very poor excuse, and is indica-
tive of an unwillingness to conscientiously try. These four
words show low self-esteem, and little trust in self and divine
assistance.

"I don't care," causes people to think that the person saying such words has lost the sense of pride, has closed the door
on the possibility of a success and lost the key to self respect
and personal independence. It means that person is willing to
be dependent on the initiative of others, or is callous and un-
concerned.

When anyone says, "I don't feel responsible; let someone
else do it," he or she is inviting the loss of both opportunity
and freedom. If we constantly leave it to others, we will be
constantly dissatisfied, acknowledging incompetence, and
abandoning our best selves. Each of us must feel responsibility or lose the virtue of self-management.

When young people say such things, it is usually because they haven't learned better yet. When older persons say them, it is usually because they have become discouraged by circumstances, lost the zest for abundant living, or have decided to become super-retirees, or just plain lazy.

We have probably all heard about the cardinal virtues of ancient Greek philosophy — justice, prudence, fortitude, and temperance. Most of us have heard of the theological virtues — hope, faith, and charity; and perhaps also the personal virtues of patience, perseverance, self-control, and chastity. The virtue of self-management goes beyond these. Its aim is to bring out the best in us, to the end that we are unwilling to say such things as: "I can't help myself." "I don't care." "I don't feel responsible; let someone else do it."

Lines from "My Kingdom," by Louisa May Alcott are well worth remembering.

> *I do not ask any crown*
> *But that which all may win;*
> *Nor try to conquer the world*
> *Except the one within.*
> *Be thou my guide until I find,*
> *Led by a tender hand,*
> *The happy kingdom of myself*
> *And dare to take command.*

The Benediction:

Now unto him who is able to keep you from falling, and to preserve you faultless before the presence of his glory with exceeding joy: to the only wise God our Savior, be glory and majesty, dominion and power, both now and ever. Amen.

The Choral Response: *(Sung by all)*

God be with you till we meet again;
By his counsel guide, uphold you;
With his sheep securely fold you;
God be with you till we meet again. Amen.

3

What Is That In Your Hand?

Instrumental Meditation

Words Of Preparation:
What is that in your hand? Perhaps your hand is holding nothing just now. For the sake of focusing on our theme, please open your hands, palm upward, and look at them. Each hand is distinctive in its markings, even to the individualization of each fingerprint, which may be copied and recorded for identity purposes. The hand is wonderfully made. No other moving part of the body has so many multiple capabilities or essential functions, such as greeting, holding, touching, and writing.

Hymn: "Guide Me, O Thou Great Jehovah"

Scripture: Exodus 4:1-5 (NRSV)
Then Moses answered, "But suppose they do not believe me or listen to me, but say, 'The Lord did not appear to you.' " The Lord said to him, "What is that in your hand?" He said, "A staff." And he said, "Throw it down on the ground." So he threw it down on the ground, and it became a snake; and Moses drew back from it. Then the Lord said to Moses, "Reach out your hand and seize it by the tail," — so he reached out his hand and grasped it, and it became a staff in his hand — "so that they may believe the Lord, the

God of our ancestors, the God of Abraham, the God of Isaac, and the God of Jacob has appeared to you."

A Prayer:

O God, we lift our hands and hearts up unto you, asking that you will guide us in the use of our hands, and how we feel about our mission in life. When tasks seem hard, grant that we may find tools to use, and insight to make our ideas work for the service of your kingdom on earth. As it was in the days of Moses, people still cry out for freedom, not only from slavery, but from ignorance and misinformation, from the pain of man's inhumanity to man, and from hunger and disease. If necessary, O Lord, put sticks in our hands with which to remind people that God is able to do all and more than we ask. When we sing, "He's got the whole world in his hands," let us not forget that you expect us to make good use of that which has been given into our hands, and that we must use it all well and wisely. This we pray in the name of our Lord Jesus the Christ. Amen.

―――――――

Sermon: "What Is That In Your Hand?"

What we receive into our hands, what we hold with them, what we give with them, what we do with them in the service of others tells much of what we are in mind and heart. The hand that writes imprints a message beyond speech. The hand that aids another speaks of caring, and of loving life. The hand that touches in greeting and friendship dissipates the void of loneliness and separation from personal and spiritual security. Our hands are to be used for gathering and for feeding, for planning and for building, for sharing and upholding, for caressing and for protecting.

William Cowper said it well when he wrote, "God moves in mysterious ways his wonders to perform." He used a stick to convince Moses and his people that they must move forward to freedom and new horizons, and to get the attention of the Pharaoh in their plea for spiritual and national release. The walking sticks of Moses and Aaron became the symbols of courage and confidence, and were reminders that God is always with his people, no matter how much difficulty they encounter.

God calls us in every age of our lives to be fully aware of that which is in our hands, and of our obligation to use all things with appropriateness, wisely, well, trustworthily, and in good conscience. Let us not forget that more often than we realize, we hold lives in our hands. When we do, they must be nurtured, protected, loved, and revered.

Moses became the great prophet of his people, and Aaron their priest. Both carried rods of wood in their hands, but more importantly, they carried love for their people and a sense of divine responsibility for their hearts, minds, and souls. So should we, especially if we are older, more experienced, and have more to love than do those who are younger. We never grow too old to love and lift the hearts and souls of others.

The Aaronic Benediction: *(May be shared in unison)*
The Lord bless you and keep you: the Lord make his face to shine upon you and be gracious to you: the Lord lift up his countenance upon you, and give you peace. Amen. (from Numbers 6:24-26)

4
What Can I Do With Who I Am?

Instrumental Meditation

Words Of Preparation Matthew 16:13-17 (TEV)

Jesus went to the territory near the town of Caesarea Philip-pi, where he asked his disciples, ''Who do people say the Son of Man is?''

''Some say, John the Baptist,'' they answered. ''Others say Elijah, while others say Jeremiah or some other prophet.''

''What about you?'' he asked them. ''Who do you say that I am?''

Simon Peter answered, ''You are the Messiah, the Son of the living God.''

''Good for you, Simon son of John!'' answered Jesus. ''For this truth did not come from any human being, but it was given directly by my Father in heaven.''

Hymn: ''Thou My Everlasting Portion''

A Prayer:

O God our Father, as we are gathered here to worship, we ask that you will abide in our midst, blessing us with under-standing, quickened hearts and minds, and feelings of godly fellowship and increasing faith. We come seeking to know what we can best do with who we are. By the counsel of your Holy Spirit, guide us we pray, to understand and to do that which

21

you want and expect of us, regardless of age, or limitations, and in keeping with our abilities and creative desires. In the same way, Fanny Crosby, the hymn writer, who though blind from infancy, was creative right up to the conclusion of her 95 years, inspires us also to be productive and giving of ourselves to the end of our days. This we humbly pray in the name of our Lord Jesus Christ. Amen.

Scripture: John 1:19-23 and 8:25-30 (NRSV)

This is the testimony given by John when the Jews sent priests and Levites from Jerusalem to ask him, "Who are you?" He confessed and did not deny it, but confessed, "I am not the Messiah." And they asked him, "What then? Are you Elijah?" He said, "I am not." "Are you the prophet?" He answered, "No." Then they said to him, "Who are you? Let us have an answer for those who sent us. What do you say about yourself?" He said,

"I am the voice of one crying out
in the wilderness,
'Make straight the way for the
Lord.' "

as the prophet Isaiah said.

They said to him, "Who are you?" Jesus said to them, "Why do you speak at all? I have much to say about you and much to condemn; but the one who sent me is true, and I declare to the world that I have heard from him." They did not understand that he was speaking to them about the Father. So Jesus said, "When you have lifted up the Son of Man, then you will realize that I am he, and I do nothing of my own, but I speak these things and the Father has instructed me. And the one who sent me is with me; he has not left me alone, for I always do what is pleasing to him." As he was saying these things, many believed in him.

22

The Sermon: "What Can I Do With Who I Am?"

Both John and Jesus were asked, "Who are you?" and in that question is also implied, "What are you doing with who you are? What is your mission in life?" There was nothing wrong in the inquiry. It opened the way for understanding John and Jesus and their work, and it gave each of them opportunity to clarify their roles in the kingdom of God.

Each of you, if asked, "Who are you?" would have your own distinctive answer. It is important that we know who we are, and what we are, but a more pressing question is, "What can I do with who I am?" It is equally important that we establish the quest for what we ought to become. Life offers many opportunities. The longer we live, the more we discover how we fit into its challenges, and we need to ask, "What can I do now with who I am?"

Mary Beth Fulton told this story. A little boy was bitterly disappointed because he could neither play nor sing. One day he told Amati, a violin maker, about his disappointment. Amati said, "Come into the house and you shall try. The song in the heart is all that matters, for there are many ways of making music. Some play violins, some sing, some paint pictures, some carve statues, while others till the soil and grow flowers. Each sings a song and helps make the music of the world. You can make music too." It was this encouragement that stimulated Antonio Stradivarius to become the world's greatest violin maker. He was never known as a great singer or virtuoso violinist, but he made the best instruments upon which the great musicians might play. He made music by creating the best violins for the artistry of the great violinists. He satisfied the question, "What can I do with who I am?"

The question, "What can I do with who I am?" does not lead to easy answers, but it does lead to the discovery of what is important now. Being a disciple involves more than belief; it also includes doing what is needful in the context of our believing. It means being our best for our own sakes, and for the sake of others. It means dedicating ourselves to the highest and best that we know in keeping with the full extent of our

23

abilities and resources. It means putting God before self at all times.

It is important that we be courageous in asking the question, "What can I do with who I am, now that I am getting old?" The answer is: do all that you can, utilizing the powers with which God has endowed you. Always, in every circumstance, endeavor to be your best.

The Benediction:

May God's richest blessings be upon each of us as we seek right answers to the question, "What can I do with who I am now?" This we ask in the name of the Lord, who has shown us the Way, the Truth, and the Life. Amen.

5
What Did You Say?

Instrumental Meditation

Words Of Preparation from Psalm 15

O Lord, who shall dwell in thy holy hill?

He who walks blamelessly, and does what is right, and speaks truth from his heart; who does not slander with his tongue, and does no evil to his friend, nor takes up reproach against his neighbor.

Hymn: "Wonderful Words Of Life"

A Brief Prayer:

Let the words of our mouths and the meditations of our hearts be acceptable in your sight, O Lord, our rock and our redeemer. Grant that we shall remember that a word fitly spoken is like apples of gold in a picture of silver. Enable us so that we may always refrain from saying anything that we might regret later, or embarrass ourselves, others, or you, Lord. Amen.

Scriptures: (NRSV)

You shall not take the name of the Lord your God in vain, for the Lord will not hold him guiltless who takes his name in vain. (Exodus 20:7)

You shall not bear false witness against your neighbor. (Exodus 20:16)

The tongue is a fire .... With it we bless the Lord and Father, and with it we curse men, who are made in the likeness of God. From the same mouth come blessing and cursing. My brethren, this ought not to be so. (James 3:6, 9-10)

Jesus said, "I tell you, every sin and blasphemy will be forgiven men, but the blasphemy against the Spirit will not be forgiven. And whoever says a word against the Son of Man will be forgiven; but whoever speaks against the Holy Spirit will not be forgiven, either in this age or in the age to come." ... "Out of the abundance of the heart the mouth speaks. The good man out of his good treasure brings forth good, and the evil man out of his evil treasure brings forth evil. I tell you, on the day of judgment men will render account for every careless word they utter; for by your words you will be justified, and by your words you will be condemned." (Matthew 12:31-32; 34b-36)

Hymn: "Just For Today"

Sermon: "What Did You Say?"

As a child, did you ever have the experience of saying something you shouldn't, see your parent or parents turn and look at you so that you felt that his or her eyes looked right through you, and then ask, "What did you say?" When that happens there is no doubt about accountability!

Words are tools for managing the machinery of life, for inspiring the soul of man, and for evaluation of the acts and motives of life; and they provide history for the understanding of humanity and life itself.

Correct words, good manners, kindly words of concern are the marks of gentility and ladyhood. All of us do well to remember that politeness is like an air cushion; there doesn't seem to be much in it, but it sure eases the jolts. Self-control in all matters, including speech, sets the tone and quality of our lives.

As a boy, if I ever uttered a swear word or a vulgarity, and my mother overheard it, my tongue received an Ivory Soap washing. It taught me that cursing and undesirable language were to be seriously avoided, and that constructive speech and expression were much better choices. A good vocabulary is a wonderful help. An English teacher once remarked, "Unwarranted expletives are the mark of a person who doesn't know how to talk, only how to make vain noises."

Talking ugly to people, making harsh demands, giving severe criticism, all make folks uncomfortable. Requests made in kindliness, and with expressed appreciation for performance well done are much more desirable. There are times when we feel uncomfortable with circumstances or behaviors, but so may those who offend, because of conditions we know nothing about. Gracious words usually make things go much easier in life. Do and say unto others as you would wish them to do and say unto you is the best practice in life. We should all remember that old age is not a valid excuse for being mean in either speech or behavior. No matter how old we become, and are consciously discerning, we are still held accountable before God for what we say and do.

We need to be aware that no matter how beneficial the words said may be, unfortunately there are those whose intention it is to hear only what they want to hear, and the only words to which they will listen are those that help to entrench their prejudices and pre-drawn conclusions. Personal stubbornness is a strange malady.

Sometimes people are worried that they may have committed the unpardonable sin. If you are worried that you may have done so, you can't have done it, simply because you are concerned that you might have. Those who are in danger are persons who are entirely indifferent to God, to spiritual values, and moral obligations. The agnostic is really in search of answers. The atheist is a protagonist. The "unpardonable sinner" is one who cares about nothing — not even enough to argue with or against God. If you are concerned about your soul's well-being you are not on the list of the "unpardonable sinners."

Several tests apply to the value of what we say. Do we honestly feel that it is true? Are we comfortable living by the words we say? Does what we say do harm to or insult others? Does what we say meet the approval of God's standards? Will our words lead others astray?

When we were young boys my brother and I were having a fun fight with feather pillows at our grandmother's home. She came in as we were doing so, and said, "Boys, if you break the pillow seams and the feathers come out of the casing, you will be responsible for picking up every one of them, and putting them back into the pillow." The fun war stopped instantly. We knew we were accountable to our grandmother.

Words said in anger, carelessly, or harmfully are much like the feathers in a pillow. If they escape, they are hard to reclaim. It is much better to be very careful what we say, and how we react to what is said. Though we may think we are safe in what we are doing, the self-encased words may break loose when we strike out at another. We are accountable to God.

The Benediction:

O God, may the words of our mouths and the meditations of our hearts always be a blessing in your sight, to others, and for ourselves. In Jesus' name we pray. Amen.

6
Expect Great Things To Happen!

Instrumental Meditation

Words Of Preparation:
In The New Revised Standard Version of the Bible the 11th chapter of The Letter to the Hebrews is headed "The Meaning of Faith." The first three verses of that chapter say, "Now faith is the assurance of things hoped for, the conviction of things not seen. Indeed by faith our ancestors received approval. By faith we understand that the worlds were prepared by the word of God, so that what is seen was made from things that were not visible."

Let us keep these truths in mind as we worship today.

Hymn: "O Master, Let Me Walk With Thee"

A Brief Prayer:
O God our Father, in reading from the gospel according to Luke 17:5, we learn that disciples said to Jesus, "Increase our faith!" That is also our plea. Lord, open our eyes, our minds, and our hearts, that we may understand and believe as we should. Instead of feeling sour about our life situations, grant us the ability to be optimistic, and to expect great things to happen and to bless our lives. This we humbly ask in the name of our Savior Jesus the Christ. Amen.

Preface to the Old Testament Reading:

Abram's nephew, Lot, had separated himself, his family, and his lifestock from Abram because of over-grazing and sustenance problems. Some tribes who resented his presence and growth, organized together, and captured him. Abram, in response, formed troops of 318 of his best men, and using good strategy soundly defeated the captors, and saved Lot.

King Melchisedek of Salem, who also served as a priest, known as priest of God Most High, brought out bread and wine, and blessed Abram, saying, "Blessed be Abram by God Most High, maker of heaven and earth; and blessed by God most High, who has delivered your enemies into your hand."

The Old Testament Reading: Genesis 15:1-6

After these things the word of the Lord came to Abram in a vision, "Do not be afraid. Abram, I am your shield; your reward shall be very great." But Abram said, "O Lord God, what will you give me, for I continue childless, and the heir of my house is Eliezer of Damascus?" And Abram said, "You have given me no offspring, and so a slave born in my house is to be my heir." But the word of the Lord came to him, "This man shall not be your heir." He brought him outside and said, "Look toward heaven and count the stars, if you are able to count them." Then he said to him, "So shall your descendants be." And he believed the Lord; and the Lord reckoned it to him as righteousness.

The Sermon: "Expect Great Things To Happen!"

Who of us has not, at some time, had the experience of feeling, that in spite of all that we have done, nothing of great importance is going to come of it. When that is the case, we often blame others, God, or ourselves as failures, and become apathetic, disgusted, or depressed. Some even have tantrums because they feel so frustrated.

It is no small wonder that Abram was disquieted. Often when a man had no direct descendant, the chief servant became the overseer of his estate. He was concerned that Ishmael, his young child by the servant girl, Hagar, would in time, become a substitute for what he most preferred. Abram might have remained in his tent, feeling sorry for himself, and allowing depression to get him down. Instead he expressed his feelings to God, and God prompted him to go outside. He heard God saying to him, "Look toward heaven and count the stars, if you are able to count them. So shall your descendants be." And he believed the Lord. He began to expect great things to happen!

A little while later, when Abram was 99 and Sarah was 90, they were told by three visitors that Sarah would have a son as promised — but Sarah laughed at the idea, after which they were confronted with God's question, "Is anything too wonderful ("hard" in KJV) for the Lord?"

Most of us have personal dreams, hopes, and goals we would like to see fulfilled. Our trouble is that we are prone to discount ourselves and our faith, and we frequently overlook the fact of God in our lives. That which may seem impossible for us may be entirely possible with God. What would you most like to see come to pass within your lifetime? What ideals have you that are well within the natural and intentional will of God, as you understand it to be, that you hope will come to fruition? Remember, "Faith is the assurance of things hoped for, the conviction of things not seen."

When outcomes seem to have been delayed, and when we want things to happen yesterday, we should not become impatient, aggravated, or take it out on others. Rather, we should be prepared, so that when our chance to celebrate life comes, we may rejoice in it.

We are God's people. We are not here as puppets of earthly pressures, or to conform to the ways of the world. We are here to be a part of the transformation of life, spiritual initiatives, personalized enrichments, and endurance in enrichments and faithfulness.

31

In that wonderful 14th chapter of John's Gospel, in which Jesus offers so much comfort to believers, there are some words from Jesus which we may overlook, that are very important. He said, "Very truly I tell you, the one who believes in me will also do the works that I do and, in fact, will do greater works than these, because I go to the Father." Upon us is bestowed a trust to do more than has ever been done before! What a challenge, for which we should do no less than our best in faith and our personal part in fulfillment!

Being old or needing care in a retirement center or a nursing home doesn't mean that we are useless or ineffectual. It may mean that we are charged with serious responsibility for inspiring those who come after us in ways that we could not otherwise accomplish.

We must expect great things to happen!

The Closing Prayer:

Gracious Lord, grant that we shall not be like the impatient servant portrayed in the 12th chapter of the Gospel according to Luke, who, when his Master was delayed in coming, became mean and dissipative, took his anger and resentment out on others, and in spite of his skills and hard work let impatience overrule his self-control. Help us to remember Jesus' words said in summary of that story: "From everyone to whom much has been given, much will be required; and from one to whom much has been entrusted, even more will be demanded." Lord, make us worthy of the trust you have placed in us. This we humbly pray. Amen.

7
With Christ As Partner

Instrumental Meditation

Words Of Preparation:
A partner is a person who takes part in some activity in common with another or others. For partners there are factors of trust and friendship. They usually have similar goals and share in the overall efforts of their endeavors. Today we think of Jesus as both partner and friend of the original disciples and of ourselves.

Hymn: "Jesus Is All The World To Me"

Scripture: Luke 5:1-11 (NRSV)
Once while Jesus was standing beside the lake of Gennesaret, and the crowd was pressing in on him to hear the word of God, he saw two boats there at the shore of the lake; the fishermen were gone out of them and were washing their nets. He got into one of the boats, the one belonging to Simon, and asked him to put out a little from the shore. Then he sat down and taught the crowds from the boat. When he had finished speaking, he said to Simon, "Put out into the deep water and let down your nets for a catch." Simon answered, "Master, we have worked all night long but have caught nothing. Yet if you say so, I will let down the nets." When they had done this, they caught so many fish that their nets were beginning

to break. So they signaled their partners in the other boat to come and help them. And they came and filled both boats, so that they began to sink. But when Simon Peter saw it, he fell down at Jesus' knees, saying, "Go away from me, Lord, for I am a sinful man!" For he and all those with him were amazed at the catch of fish they had taken; and so also were James and John, sons of Zebedee, who were partners with Simon. Then Jesus said to Simon, "Do not be afraid; from now on you will be catching people." When they had brought their boats to shore, they left everything and followed him.

Sermon: "With Christ As Partner"

Though it was early in Jesus' ministry, crowds were already beginning to gather and to follow him wherever he went. They were eager for his personal interest and ministry to their particular needs. Jesus knew that there was more to ministering to people than the acts of pastoral care and compassion. Without basic learning through teaching and preaching, spiritual foundations are hard to lay and concepts of enduring meaning are neglected.

Jesus had earlier made friends with Peter when his brother Andrew brought him to meet Jesus at his residence, according to a story found in John 2:35-42. On that occasion he saw great potential in Peter, and called him "the Rock." It seems natural that he would use Peter's boat to separate himself enough from the press of the people to do some meaningful teaching for all to hear. His discourse did not stop the fishermen from washing and stretching their nets, or from hearing what he was saying. Evidently Jesus' message lasted until Peter brought his nets back to the boat.

Jesus remained in the boat, and suggested that a try be made for a catch. Peter was surprised by the proposal, because an all-night effort had been unsuccessful, but if Jesus said so, they would try. Together Peter and Jesus put out the nets in deeper water away from the shore, and on the first try the nets were filled to over-flowing, requiring that Peter call for help from his fishing partners, James and John, the sons of Zebedee. They brought their boat, and both craft were filled with so many fish that they were threatened with sinking, but they managed to get safely back to shore. Peter, in remorse for his doubt and behavior, knelt before Jesus, and confessed his feelings of unworthiness. Jesus in a short time had become a friend, a partner, and spiritual leader for these fishermen. To their further amazement and surprise he invited them to become his partners in a new enterprise — fishing for people — and they left everything and followed him.

What happened to the great catch of fish? Was Zebedee left with responsibility for preparing and taking them for sale? Was the crowd invited to take what they needed for themselves for fresh food at home? We aren't told. But we do know that Peter, James, and John were from that moment on close partners with Jesus in his Messianic mission. It was they who took the initiative in the formation of the early church after the events of the crucifixion and resurrection of Jesus the Christ.

The identification of a person as a Christian proclaims a partnership with Christ. That person is supposed to have spiritual resources that the secular world can never give. The Christian is not set apart from the world, but in the midst of it becomes an influence in doing good, rather than surrendering to secularized conformity.

Christ as partner always bears his share and more in all responsibilities of Christian endeavor. The greatest partnership anyone ever forms is that of the Christian covenant. It is backed by the institution known as the church, through which spiritual profits are channeled. It is the greatest business in the world, because mankind is constantly wanting religious service and better ways in which to serve.

Futility and triviality are not a part of the Christian mission. There is genuine concern about the most pressing issues of society and humanity's needs. Progress is continual, and growth is a priority. If you want a partner who can make your life a real success, choose Christ. With him there are no regretful relationships, no bankruptcy of spirit, no moral corruption, and the net gains are wonderful, for they always add up to eternal life, if we are found faithful in performing our part in the partnership, which is a reasonable and sacred commitment of life and service. We are never too old or disabled to become a partner with Christ.

A Prayer:

Thank you, God for this wonderful story of men who became partners with Christ. It does our hearts and souls good when we realize the wonders and joys of our partnership with him as our Lord and leader in life. Sometimes we are prone to forget and fail in doing our part, for which we are ashamed, and like Peter, ask your forgiveness for our personal failures. Teach us how to be good fishers of men, and to rejoice in catching them, even as we have been caught for the kingdom of God. Amen.

8
If We Are Dreamers

Instrumental Meditation

The Call To Worship:
Let us give thanks to the Lord for his steadfast love, for his wonderful works to the sons of men!

Yours, O Lord, is the greatness, and the power, and the glory, and the victory, and the majesty; for all that is in the heavens and in the earth is yours; yours is the kingdom, O Lord, and you are exalted as head above all.

Bless our God, O people, let the sound of his praise be heard. Amen.

Hymn: "O Worship The King!"

The Prayer Of Invocation:
O Eternal God, speak to each of us the word that we need, and let your word abide with us until it has wrought in us your holy will. We humbly ask that you will cleanse our minds, quicken our spirits, and refresh our hearts. Direct and increase our faith. May we in our worship at this time be enabled to envision your spirit more clearly, to love you more completely, and to serve you more perfectly; through Jesus Christ our Lord. Amen.

Scripture: Joel 2:27, 28; also found in Acts 2:17 (NRSV)
I, the Lord, am your God and there is no other.

I will pour out my spirit on all flesh; and your sons and your daughters shall prophesy, your old men shall dream dreams, and your young men shall see visions.

Hymn: "Dear Master, In Whose Life I See"

Sermon: "If We Are Dreamers"

There are many kinds of dreams, among them normal sleep dreams, daydreams, and insightful visions. Sometimes we have nightmares, fantasies, re-living of moments in life, happy dreams, reunions with loved ones, even problem-solving or inspirational dreams.

It is helpful for us to be aware of what dreams are: the subconscious feelings or imaginations occurring just below the threshold of consciousness. We need to find means for dealing with dreams that disturb us, by discovery of means for dealing with them in ways of appropriate conscious understanding and sensible disposal.

A boy in his preschool until young adult years had a frequent nightmare in which he would be on a railroad track over an elevated earthen mound. Suddenly a train would come over the horizon, and he would do his best to run away from it. No matter how fast he ran, he couldn't get away from it, and the cow-catcher nipped at his heels. When he felt he could run no more, he would suddenly wake up in a cold sweat. As a young adult, he knew there must be a reason for this recurrent dream, so he searched his memory, and recalled that when he was about five years old, a newborn calf strayed from its mother, got on a cattle guard about a quarter mile from his grandfather's house, and was run over by a fast-moving train. When the train had passed, he went to see what happened to the calf. The tragedy was imprinted in his young mind and he would subconsciously run from the train, as he hoped the calf might have done. When he realized the cause of his bad dream, it never occurred again. The clear light of reason and understanding relieved the subconscious fear that haunted him.

38

Perhaps the most classic of dreams were those of Joseph, the son of Jacob, as recounted in Genesis 37. His brothers, being jealous of him and his grandiose recounting of the dreams of superiority, sold him into slavery. Strangely the dreams came true some years later when his family was driven into Egypt by famine in their native land. The story is well worth reading beginning with the 37th and concluding with the 47th chapter of Genesis, too long to be fully recounted here.

There are conscious dreams in life that stem from hope, ambition, and the need to serve. That is the meaning of the dreams alluded to in the hymn we shared, written by John Hunter. Those were the kinds of dreams that Jesus treasured and sought to help to fulfillment. Dreams should cause us to reflect on what has been, what ought to be, and what our role in life is to become. Reflective memories are precious to us, but ultimate outcomes are even more so.

Shepherds was an inspirational magazine that was in circulation in the late 1940s. This article, titled "My Dream," appeared in the magazine. It was written by Hugh O. Isbell, then pastor of St. Paul's Methodist Church in Springfield, Missouri.

I dreamed last night — it must have been a day-dream — that there had gone out a decree from the Ruler of the universe that for 10 years the stars would shine no more. That night the world was full of sad and wakeful people. The streets were crowded with them driving to some country scene to get a last longing look. Mothers awakened their babies, too young to know the significance of what was going on, hoping that they could at least gain some impression. And for the whole long night, people who had seldom lifted their eyes to look at the stars sat up and looked until the last star faded into the brightening day. Well did one say, "If the stars shone only once in 10 years, we would sit up all night to look at them."

I dreamed also that laughter had been banished for 10 years. One day was granted before the decree should be enforced, but on that day nobody laughed. The prospect of having no laughter as medicine for the heart had already banished joy.

In this dream there was also a ban on beauty. The leaves of autumn were commanded to die and fall without their manifold coloring. Spring was commanded not to return, and winter was forbidden to paint the landscape; and many people cried, "If beauty dies, let me die too. Without roses, autumn woods, and spring, and the beauty of human faces, life is not worth living." But many of these had never lifted a note of praise to God for all the beauty of the world.

And last of all, I looked and saw a mighty lock on every church, and a poster forbidding anyone to sing or pray or worship God. Then I saw people leaning against the walls weeping, and walking about in sadness, and the powers of evil grinning, and mothers saying, "Cursed be the day I brought a child into such a world."

Then I awoke and thanked God it was only a dream, and promised God I would take time to look at the stars, and enjoy and create beauty, and laugh, and worship.

Dreams sometimes awaken in us needed responses to life situations and dangers. Matthew 2:12-13 speaking of the wise men, reads, "And being warned in a dream that they should not return to Herod, they departed to their own country by another way. And when they departed, behold the angel of the Lord appeareth to Joseph in a dream, saying, 'Arise and take the young child and his mother, and flee into Egypt, and be thou there until I bring thee word: for Herod will seek the young child to destroy him.' " (KJV)

Whether our dreams serve to warn us, to inspire us, to help us in solving problems; as a reflection of the enjoyment of life and pleasant memories, or to help us in the fulfillment of a hope, ambition, or the need to serve; let us thank God for dreams, and for the waking hours in which to deal with remembered dreams and duties alike. And old people can dream dreams as well as anyone else. Why not? They add a sense of excitement to life.

The Benedictory Hymn: "God Be With You Till We Meet Again"

9
The Beauty
Of Holiness

Instrumental Meditation

A Call To Worship: *(May be said or sung)*
O worship the Lord in the beauty of holiness;
Serve him with gladness all the earth. Amen!

Hymn: "Take Time To Be Holy"

A Prayer Of Invocation:
Our gracious heavenly Father, humbly we invoke your
blessing upon us for this time of worship. We know that your
name is synonymous with love, that your nature is compassion, that your presence brings joy, that your Word is truth,
your spirit is goodness, your holiness is beauty, your will is
peace, in your service is perfect freedom, and by faith in you
through Jesus Christ your Son we are assured of life eternal.
Unto you, O Lord, be all honor and glory, now and for evermore. Amen.

Scriptures: Psalm 96:1-3; 9-11a (KJV)
O sing unto the Lord a new song: sing unto the Lord,
all the earth.
Sing unto the Lord, bless his name; show forth his
salvation from day to day.
Declare his glory among the heathen, his wonders among
all people. . . .

worship the Lord in the beauty of holiness; fear
before him all the earth.
Say among the heathen that the Lord reigneth: the
world also shall be established that it shall
not be moved: he shall judge the people
righteously.
Let the heavens rejoice, and let the earth be glad.

Hymn: "Jesus Shall Reign"

Sermon: "The Beauty Of Holiness"

The 96th Psalm is closely comparable with 1 Chronicles
16:23-26. Psalm 29:2 also contains the words, "Worship the
Lord in the beauty of holiness." The New Revised Standard
Version translated Psalm 96:9 to read, "Worship the Lord in
holy splendor; tremble before him all the earth." Older people have long been accustomed to using the words from the
King James Version.

Worship ought to be made beautiful in sight, sound, and
thought. The physical settings of worship experiences serve to
enhance and reinforce the yearning for understanding and com-
pleteness. This may be illustrated by a question: "Would you
rather have a picnic on a graveled area in the heat of the sun,
or where there is verdure of grass, and the shade of trees?"
Worship is best when the scene is not barren, but blessed with
good architecture, beauty of color, protection from the elements, and in the presence of an altar, giving it sacred significance.

We need to remember that truth is not only conveyed by
words. It is also shared in feelings, situational inclusion, comfortable meditation and contemplation, which nurtures us. But
worship can also take place in foxholes of distress, danger,
and despair. God's messages and our responses do not always
come in pretty packages with liturgical decorations. Sometimes
they come in moments of destitution, hunger, inner distress,

pain, and loneliness. What we make of what we learn at such times turns the place of discovery into a temple, and we worship in the beauty of holiness because we have found a relationship that truly enriches life.

Worship may take place in prison, a hospital or a nursing home; in a cemetery, a forest, or in a barren desert. It was in a desert setting that Jesus dealt with his temptations and life determinations, as he recalled Deuteronomy 6:13, and declared, "You shall worship the Lord your God, and him only shall you serve." To the woman at the well in Samaria, Jesus said, "Believe me the hour is coming when on this mountain nor in Jerusalem will you worship the Father. ... But the hour is coming, and now is, when the true worshipers will worship the Father in spirit and truth, for such the Father seeks to worship him. God is a spirit, and those who worship him must worship in spirit and in truth." (See John 4:19-24)

All of us yearn for the experience of "worship in the beauty of holiness." The psychiatrist, Von Frankl, held that the urge to worship is instinctive in children in much the same way as the urge to nurse. He suggested that the ages of four and five are the times when children are most desirous and accepting for the experiences of worship. Esthetics and quality appreciation are important to the development and life of the child. The elderly demonstrate much of the same needs in their lives.

"The beauty of holiness" is a most suggestive and satisfying phrase. It conveys the idea of "Holy Presence," and of being involved in spiritual goodness. My how human hearts long for that! In the midst of crassness, competitiveness, controversies, hostility, and uncertainty of conditions, we need that respite desperately.

Symbolism, the historic sign of faith, serves to renew our sense of oneness with what has been generative before us, and proclaims that we too can be involved in the experience of personal inclusion.

The building we refer to as the church or the chapel ought to be as adequate, as comfortable, and as attractive as we want our homes to be. Shouldn't God's house be the most attractive and architecturally satisfying of all?

43

Nostalgia is important to many of us, and plays a tremendous role in our religious and personal life. It is the incentive that leads us to memorialize — to provide new and beautiful things that relate to worship. Yet, we know that nostalgic sentiment can become a barrier to doing what is most important for the future. We can become so attached to what we have, and give our loyalty to what is familiar, that we may neglect to see what we ought to develop.

"The beauty of holiness" should inspire us for the transformation of life. It should also challenge us to greater things, with God's encouragement and guidance. Contemplating "the beauty of holiness" is not enough! We must also ask, "And what else ought we to do, God?" The answer we receive may not be the one we might prefer, but we had better not pray, "Thy will be done," unless we are willing to be a part of that will. God calls us to the faithful application of our Christian belief and commitment to discipleship, in which is included "the beauty of holiness." Therein lies the great truth of the words with which we began this worship time:

"O worship the Lord in the beauty of holiness;
Serve him with gladness all the earth." Amen.

The Benediction:

Send us forth, O God, causing us to remember that the beauty of holiness needs to show in our lives, through Jesus Christ our Lord. Amen.

10
With Unwavering Trust

Instrumental Meditation

The Call To Worship: *(By the leader)*
"The Lord is in his holy temple;
Let all the earth keep silence
    before him." Amen.

The Instrumental Prelude: *(People reverently silent)*

Scripture: Romans 4:13-25 (NRSV)

The promise that he would inherit the world did not come to Abraham or his descendants through the law but through the righteousness of faith. If it is the adherents of the law who are to be heirs, faith is null and the promise is void. For the law brings wrath; but where there is no law, neither is there violation.

For this reason it depends on faith, in order that the promise may rest on grace and be guaranteed to all his descendants, not only to adherents of the law but also those who share the faith of Abraham (for he is the father of all of us, as it is written, "I have made you the father of many nations") — in the presence of God in whom he believed, who gives life to the dead and calls into existence things that do not exist. Hoping against hope, he believed that he would become "the father of many nations," according to what was said, "So numerous

45

shall your descendants be." He did not weaken in faith when he considered his own body, which was already as good as dead (for he was about a hundred years old), or when he considered the barrenness of Sarah's womb. No distrust made him waiver concerning the promise of God, but he grew strong in his faith as he gave glory to God, being fully convinced that God was able to do what he had promised. Therefore his faith "was reckoned to him as righteousness." Now the words, "it was reckoned to him," were written not for his sake alone, but for ours also. It will be reckoned to us who believe in him who raised Jesus our Lord from the dead, who was handed over to death for our trespasses and was raised for our justification.

Hymn: "A Charge To Keep I Have"

Sermon: "With Unwavering Trust"

As we increase in the accumulation of years, and our bodies and personal resolves seem to weaken, we may find it difficult to keep the promises of God in mind. We may even find ourselves staggering, wavering, faltering, and discounting our ultimate goals of faith and endeavor. But Abraham did not, though he was old, and his example is good for us. Those of us who are older persons, may find it difficult to remain enthusiastic and determined. We may be tempted to consider giving up before we should because faithfulness and energetic persistence are not easy for us, either physically or mentally.

Dr. Frank Delitzch, of Leipzig University, who lived 1813-1890, was a German Hebraist and Bible critic. He was known as the founder of what is called higher criticism, and he passed from strict Lutheranism to a position near the radical critics. He issued revised texts of many of the Old Testament books, and a translation of the New Testament into Hebrew.

At one time he said to his students, "Young men, the battle is now raging around the Old Testament. Soon it will pass into the New Testament field and is already beginning there.

46

Finally, it will press forward to the citadel of our faith, the person of Jesus Christ. There the last struggle will occur. I shall not be here then, but some of you will. Be true to Christ; stand up for him, preach Christ and him crucified."

More than a century has passed since Dr. Delitzch died. We have seen many struggles in the studies of Bible and theology — but Christ still prevails!

Justification by faith is a good and wholesome doctrine, and is the key to salvation by grace; but it leads naturally to the justification of ourselves by works. While it is true that "Faith without works is dead," we must never allow works to supplant, or substitute for faith, toward which we might easily be prone. Paul taught that Jesus "was delivered (to the cross) for our offenses, and was raised for our justification." (Romans 4:25)

The purpose of orders of worship, rituals of faith and sacrament, processes of religious education and spiritual growth, is to arouse in us a favorable climate for the reception and transmission of the Christian message, and subsequent performance in life.

The basic condition for a person to be religious is to assume the reality of God — then give God an opportunity to prove the man. The promises that God gives us may stagger our imagination. The danger is that we may lose sight of God while trying to keep sight of the promises. It could have been said of Abraham, Moses, Gideon, Amos, Christ, or Paul, that each of them was in the minority, and that there was not ample reason for any of them to put out such great effort for their causes, but they would not exchange the fact of God for the promises of man's favor; they preferred the promises of God.

P. T. Barnum was not only a great showman, but also something of a philosopher. It was he who observed that more people were humbugged into believing too little than were humbugged into believing too much. The greatest danger is that people may be humbugged into believing nothing.

There is an old legend that when Peter was preaching following the ascension, if he heard the crowing of a rooster, he would be overcome for a moment with embarrassment and confusion. Then he would recover, and preach with renewed zest, more tenderly, earnestly, and convincingly than before.

We need to remember these words from Romans 4:20: "No distrust made him waver concerning the promise of God, but he grew strong in his faith as he gave glory to God, being fully convinced that God was able to do what he had promised."

May we also not waver, but more certainly than ever lay hold on the promises of God, and go on to victory every day of our lives, regardless of age, infirmity, or unexpected events! We need to remember that there is life beyond this earthly journey. We can't afford to blame the circumstances of this life for our failure to obtain the promise of eternal life.

Closing Prayer:

O God, we are aware that it would be so easy for us to slip through the cracks that appear in our faith. Make us alert to the dangers of apathy and neglect. Strengthen our resolve and enrich our perseverance that we may win over weakness, and find courage to do what we know we must to fulfill your trust in us, as well as attain the promise of eternal life. In the name of Jesus Christ our Lord. Amen.

11
Everyone Is Searching

Instrumental Meditation

Words Of Preparation: from Deuteronomy 4:29; James 4:8, 10.

"If with all your hearts ye truly seek me, ye shall surely find me;" thus saith our God.

"Draw near to God and he will draw near to you. Humble yourselves before the Lord, and he will lift you up." (KJV)

The Prayer Of Invocation:

Almighty God, author of eternal light: Illumine our hearts by the light of your grace, that our lips may praise you, that our lives may bless you, and that our worship may glorify you; through Jesus Christ our Lord. Amen.

The Lord's Prayer: *(Prayed from memory, by everyone)*

Scripture: Mark 1:35-39 (NRSV)

In the morning, while it was still very dark, he (Jesus) got up and went out to a deserted place, and there he prayed. And Simon and his companions hunted for him. When they found him, they said to him, "Everyone is searching for you." He answered, "Let us go on to the neighboring towns, so that I may proclaim the message there also; for that is what I came out to do." And he went throughout Galilee, proclaiming the message in their synagogues and casting out demons.

49

Hymn: "Holy Spirit, Faithful Guide"

Sermon: "Everyone Is Searching"

Mr. Wittenberg was an elderly man, living on a ranch. He decided to go for a walk, and somehow became disoriented, and was lost for two days on land that was ordinarily familiar to him. Everyone who lived nearby set about looking for him. They feared for his well-being, and sought to find him in hopes of saving him from unnecessary pain or death. They finally found him asleep in the shade of a clump of bushes. He was tired and hungry, but seemed otherwise in good shape, for which everyone was thankful.

The disciples were unaware of Jesus going out so early in the morning. He was desirous of peace and quiet, so went to a place that people seldom came to sit and think. When the disciples awoke and found him missing, they were concerned, and as others had also come to talk with him, everyone was searching for him. When they at last discovered where he was, they remarked, "Everyone is searching for you."

Though not always consciously, all the world looks for Jesus, because there is great need for such a person as he. All of us are searching for something, though we are not sure just what it is that we are looking for, and it is possible that we may not recognize it when we find it. Most of us want peace for our souls, respect for our standards, and hope for our futures. Some have learned that ambition and hard work are not of themselves sufficient. The reality is that grace is needed if life is to be spiritually and physically fulfilling.

They were looking for Jesus because he had a helpful message for their ears and hearts, and a ministry to meet the issues and needs of their lives and circumstances. The people realized that Jesus united his preaching with works, and his faith with action. His was not a scholarly treatise of theology. He gave evidence of faith and power with God, not mere dogma about God. They searched for him because "he taught

50

them as one with authority, and not as the scribes." He was able to rebuke evil influences in a man, so that his personality evidenced the spiritual change that had taken place.

They were eager to find him because his conversations and ministries had the ring of fresh and meaningful thought. Some of what he said stemmed from old ideas, but he gave them the ring of new truth. People sought him out because he not only brought physical and spiritual relief, but because he also put people to serving in creative ways as they ought. He was always positive in his treatment and in his purpose.

They searched for him because he not only restored confidence in people, but because he possessed genuine confidence by means of faith and prayer. He knew that his work would stand on its own merits. That should be true for all of us. This was no sensational dramatic device or psychological trick that he practiced. He got his power and his message from God the Father, and he reported to him on how things went, and he inquired about how he might plan for the greatest advantage for the kingdom's good.

People felt a need for him because he had a passion for souls, and practiced compassion for persons of every status level. He instilled in others a sense of their own need for a deep personal faith.

We know that as Christians, in imitation of the Master, it becomes our privilege to share a vital message, to maintain and utilize the power and authority of faith; and to demonstrate that confidence and devotional pattern that declares to the world, "This is it. We have found the Master, and the abundant life which he has promised for those who believe."

When they found Jesus, they realized that he had been praying about what should be done next. He told them that he and the disciples must go to the neighboring towns. It was time to spread the good news beyond where they lived. In order to keep the Christ we must share him with others.

A Closing Prayer:

O God, in searching for the Christ, we discover that our faith and concepts are enriched. We also learn that we can't keep him confined to a given locale, for his mission and ministry is universal. We are glad that he invites us to go with him wherever there is need for the Christian message and service to humanity, even right where we live. Some of us are unable to go far physically, but our prayers and our spirits can go everywhere with your help in Christ's service. Enable us, O Father, to do the best we can with what we are and can share. In Jesus' name. Amen.

12
Do You Want To Be More Spiritual?

Instrumental Meditation: *(The congregation reverently quiet)*

A Prayer Of Preparation:
Almighty God, our heavenly Father, receive us in this time of worship, as we offer ourselves anew to you in body, soul, and mind. Let not this day pass except it leave its benediction with us. Give us the still and trusting heart. Speak to us your truth, that we may be enabled to better glorify you by our lives. Grant that we become more deeply spiritual persons, through Jesus Christ our Lord. Amen.

Hymn: "In The Garden"

Scripture: Romans 8:1-11 (NRSV)
There is therefore now no condemnation for those who are in Christ Jesus. For the law of the Spirit of life in Christ Jesus has set you free from the law of sin and death. For God has done what the law, weakened by the flesh, could not do: by sending his own Son in the likeness of sinful flesh, and to deal with sin, he condemned sin in the flesh, so that the just requirement of the law might be fulfilled in us, who walk not according to the flesh but according to the Spirit. For those who live according to the flesh set their minds on the things of the flesh, but those who live according to the Spirit set their minds on the things of the Spirit. To set the mind on the

flesh is death, but to set the mind on the Spirit is life and peace. For this reason the mind that is set on the flesh is hostile to God; it does not submit to God's law — indeed it cannot, and those who are in the flesh cannot please God.

But you are not in the flesh; you are in the Spirit, since the Spirit of God dwells in you. Anyone who does not have the Spirit of Christ does not belong to him. But if Christ is in you, though the body is dead because of sin, the Spirit is life because of righteousness. If the Spirit of him who raised Jesus from the dead dwells in you, he who raised Christ from the dead will give life to your mortal bodies also through the Spirit that dwells in you.

Sermon: "Do You Want To Be More Spiritual?"

In his letter to the Philippians, Paul advised, "Let the same mind be in you that was in Christ Jesus." To the Romans he wrote, "To set the mind on the Spirit is life and peace." In order to be more spiritual, the mind needs to be fixed on abiding by the rules of spirituality. Our attitude toward God and Jesus Christ in spiritual matters, and in secular conduct has much to do with how we qualify spiritually. Our devotional, intentionally creative and conscientious participation help to enrich our spiritual manifestations.

The first requirement is to overcome the feelings of distance and strangeness in our relation to God. There are those who feel that God is aloof, or far from them, in spite of our being taught that God is everywhere. Someone asked, "When you feel far from God, who moved?" We need a working and conversational relationship with God, at least daily. Someone also asked, "Do you treat God like your doctor, only consulting with him when you have a problem?"

Learn to use prayer as an instrument of faith, rather than as a salve for conscience, or a plea in emergencies. We should, instead of praying out of duty, talk with God out of love for him and for the life he has given us. Be willing to be yourself with God, facing the truth as it really is, letting him guide you in knowledge and understanding.

Take stock of yourself, your interests and goals in life, and talk them over with God. You may do well to share them also with a good friend who has a deep reverence for life and for God. Ask yourself if what you think and feel would have the endorsement of Jesus. Are you about to do what you sincerely believe is right under the circumstance and proper at the time? Are you putting off what you know ought to be considered because it may require more of you than you want to give of yourself, time, or substance? It is hard to feel spiritual comfort, or to be satisfied within yourself if these matters cannot be rightly dealt with.

We need to take our emotions and our reasoning both into account. Sometimes we are torn between the two. While matters of the heart are necessary to enjoy fulfillment, the mind must be in agreement, or an inner argument can ensue, causing regret for a long time. Spiritual joy dies when conflicts are not properly resolved. Remember, life is very personal, and resolution of feelings and problems are essential to spiritual growth.

Most people discover that when they have done the right thing, and have done their best in the interest of spiritual development and religious growth, inner peace comes to their lives. It is then that they come to full appreciation of the words, "To be spiritually minded is life and peace." Total commitment to God through Christ is the best means of finding that life and peace.

When we are truly spiritual persons we often find that we have considerable influence on others. These lines may well serve as our prayer.

May every soul that touches mine,
Be it the slightest contact, get therefrom some good,
Some little grace, one kindly thought,
One aspiration yet unfelt, one bit of courage
For the darkening sky, one gleam of faith

To brave the thickening ills of life;
One glimpse of brighter sky beyond the gathering mist,
to make this life worthwhile
And heaven a surer heritage. Amen.

A Closing Hymn: "Spirit Of The Living God"

13
He Came Seeking Fruit

Instrumental Meditation

Words To Start Our Meditation:
Jesus said, "I am the vine, you are the branches. By this my Father is glorified, that you bear much fruit, and so prove to be my disciples."

He also said, "Every tree that does not bear good fruit is cut down and thrown in the fire. Thus you will know them by their fruits."

Moments Of Quiet Meditation: *(Accompanied by soft music)*

Scripture: Luke 13:6-9 (NRSV)
Then he told this parable: "A man had a fig tree planted in his vineyard; and he came looking for fruit on it and found none. So he said to the gardener, 'See here! For three years I have come looking for fruit on this fig tree, and still I find none. Cut it down! Why should it be wasting the soil?' He replied, 'Sir, let it alone for one more year, until I dig around it and put manure on it. If it bears fruit next year, well and good; but if not, you can cut it down.' "

Hymn: "Open My Eyes, That I May See"

Sermon: "He Came Seeking Fruit"

Grapes were the main crop on this farm. The fig tree was planted in the vineyard, apparently because the owner wanted to enjoy some figs each year. Because the fig tree had been there at least three years, he felt that it should have borne at least some fruit, but none appeared. Nothing is said about whether the little wasp so necessary for pollinating figs, was there. Perhaps there were none of them around. It appears that the gardener felt that he may not have done all he could to help it to produce. It must be acknowledged that his first responsibility was to care for the grape vines. It may have been that he had not given much thought or attention to this lone fig tree, and felt that its failure to produce was his fault.

The tree had been planted there by the owner's instruction. Now, as he took inventory of how his farm was producing, he began to wonder if the room the fig tree required, in which several grape vines could be planted, was not unwise and unproductive use of the soil. A large fig can take up a considerable amount of ground in the expanse of its branches and large leaves. The climate in Palestine is very similar to that in Texas, and is conducive to the production of that kind of fruit tree.

The owner brought knowledgeable, experienced help to care for his vineyard and fig tree. The owner wanted the benefit of one who knew how to do what was needed, and he entrusted his crop to his supervision and care. When the time came to evaluate, the two of them talked it over, and the gardener prevailed concerning giving the tree another chance. Though the landlord was ready to pronounce immediate judgment, the vinedresser interceded, saying, "Let it alone for one more year, until I dig around it and put manure on it. If it bears fruit next year, well and good; but if not, you can cut it down."

A parablee is a teaching tool. The symbolism here sounds very much like God is the owner, and Jesus is the advocate, saying, "Give it another chance." God expects each of us to be accountable for the character of our lives and what they produce. Jesus was sent by God, with the purpose of providing us with a Redeemer, one who is interested in providing us a way to receive merciful judgment. Sinners, with the help of God's Son, may be helped to renewed life in spite of failure to have borne good fruit. The work of redeeming the tree involved corrective nurture and even discipline, including pruning. The same may apply to human beings, who are children of God.

Even if the tree was helped to bear fruit at the next inspection, meeting the owner's satisfaction, it eventually would age beyond productivity, and die, necessitating its eventual removal. The same is true for people, but maturity and death are considered normal processes of life, rather than judgmental action. This parable was about a tree, but its truths apply to people. It was Jesus' way of imprinting truth by storytelling. It has a wonderful message, for which all of us should be glad.

The Closing Prayer:

Thank you, Lord, for providing us with such a potent parable that affords us fresh hope for our lives. We rejoice that you care so much for us that you gave up your life on earth to give us hope of renewal here, and eternal life to follow. We desire to produce ample and good fruit as long as we possibly can, and pray your tender mercy upon us so long as we are alive here, then bless us also in the life which is eternal. These things we humbly ask. Amen.

14
Strong Faith For
Weak People

Instrumental Meditation

Some Thoughts To Meditate Upon:
Robert Browning wrote: "I count life just a stuff to try the soul's strength on."

Calvin Coolidge said: "The strength of a country is the strength of its religious convictions."

St. Frances de Sales held that: "Nothing is so strong as gentleness; nothing so gentle as real strength."

Psalm 46 begins: "God is our strength, a very present help in trouble."

Psalm 27:1 tells us: "The Lord is my light and my salvation; whom shall I fear? The Lord is the strength of my life; of whom shall I be afraid?"

Moments Of Silent Meditation: *(With soft instrumental music)*

A Prayer For Strength In Our Lives:
Almighty God, we humbly ask that you perpetually visit us with your strengthening Spirit, enabling us to serve you without fear. Grant unto us that love which casts out fears. Deliver us from the fear of those who hate goodness, from fear of discomfort and poverty, from fear of dreaded ills and unknown futures, from fear of our own inner weaknesses, and the dread of those mysteries of life that we do not understand.

Instill in us confidence for victorious living and adventurous souls. These things we humbly ask in the name of our Lord Jesus the Christ. Amen.

Scripture: Romans 14:1-9 (NRSV)

Welcome those who are weak in faith, but not for the purpose of quarreling over opinions. Some believe in eating anything, while the weak eat only vegetables. Those who eat must not despise those who abstain, and those who abstain must not pass judgment on those who eat; for God has welcomed them. Who are you to pass judgment on servants of another? It is before their own Lord that they stand or fall. And they will be upheld for the Lord is able to make them stand.

Some judge one day to be better than another, while others judge all days to be alike. Let all be fully convinced in their own minds. Those who observe the day, observe it in honor of the Lord. Also those who eat, eat in honor of the Lord, since they give thanks to God; while those who abstain, abstain in honor of the Lord and give thanks to God.

We do not live to ourselves, and we do not die to ourselves. If we live, we live to the Lord and if we die, we die to the Lord; so then, whether we live or whether we die, we are the Lord's. For to this end Christ died and lived again, so that he might be Lord of both the dead and the living.

Hymn: "Rise Up, O Men Of God"
(Note: "Ye saints" may be substituted for "O men")

Sermon: "Strong Faith For Weak People"

Two verses stand out in this scripture reading: "Welcome those who are weak in faith, but not for the purpose of quarreling over opinions." . . . "Let all be fully convinced in their own minds." (vv. 1, 6)

In the early fellowship of the church, extended knowledge and understanding of the faith was not as tolerant or as ecumenical as it is now, when we have a better educated clergy, and uniform organized learning systems. Many hairsplitting matters arose to vex the fellowship, and over these many stumbled. This was especially so when they sought to deal with the cosmopolitan and Gentile communities, under the reign of their several cultures. Variant sects and systems emerged because not everyone had learned the need for simple and practical applications of the faith. Often there were those who were more interested in growing feeder roots than deepening tap roots for the tree of Christianity. They failed to understand the importance of the central facts of belief, and diverted to peripheral matters.

There was in a certain congregation a very devoted Christian whom people sought to avoid, because though he had a fine education, he lacked the good common sense to leave off continually posing some kind of philosophical or religious argument. His learning prevented his stressing the graciousness that is in simple things. He somehow had missed the words of Paul, "Welcome those who are weak in faith, but not for the purpose of quarreling over opinions." Strength lies not in being all-knowing, but in being a caring person, who is familiar with the strength that comes from being Christ-like, loving, and mutually concerned.

We need to remember that God welcomes all persons into his kingdom regardless of their strengths or weaknesses. He expects us who are experienced Christians to supply the spiritual warmth that will satisfy their human longings, and add zest for life and growth discoveries.

Everyone should be careful about passing judgment on the ideas and practices of others. Sometimes, we who have been in the habit of practicing our faith and acts of life in established ways may have allowed our vision to become clouded. We need to explore fresh ideas in order to assess their value. Remember the church at Jerusalem had considerable difficulty accepting Gentile inclusion, and especially those who were baptized but not circumcised. Sometimes we need to distinguish between the value of custom as compared with expedient change in matters of faith.

In Christ there is abiding strength for all situations and considerations, because he imparts grace and spiritual power, even in times of personal weakness. With him there is no limit or barrier to faith, or special requirements for social, economic, political or ecclesiastical standing. We need to remember the words of Paul: "Let all be fully convinced in their own minds." Christian belief and practice is a matter of personal conviction, rather than imposed status symbols. Nothing is much worse than the wishy-washy person, who has no character norm, and whose judgment has but one criteria: "What's most popular?" The important thing is that what we believe and do to be holy unto God, and an honor unto Jesus Christ our Savior.

We are all bound together as a common whole, not by choice, but by natural order, and in keeping with the wisdom of God. It is as Paul said, "We do not live to ourselves, and we do not die to ourselves." We need to remember that as Christians, "We live to the Lord, and if we die, we die to the Lord; so then, whether we live or whether we die, we are the Lord's." That is what matters most. Let us not forget that all that we do affects someone else, even if done in privacy. Sooner or later we are found out to be what we are in private as well as in public. Of one thing we can be sure: God always knows.

Those among us who are strong in the faith should seek to strengthen those who are weak, through association, sympathetic conversation and service, right example, and to stand firm when great decisions are at stake. Much good can be done by abstaining from doubtful practices. Little can be accomplished by entering into argument with either social or religious fanatics. We need to remember that seldom are we able to win people for Christ by magnifying their faults; neither should they be condoned for the sake of avoiding unpleasantness. We need to be honest with everyone, while avoiding the snares of bigotry, super self-righteousness, and unseasoned counsel. Edgar A. Guest said it well when he wrote:

I'd rather see a sermon than hear one any day.
I'd rather one should walk with me than merely tell the
way.
The eye's a better pupil and more willing than the ear,
fine counsel is confusing but example's always clear.
And the best of all the preachers are the men who live
their creeds,
For to see good in action is what everybody needs.

Faith is something more meaningful for all people when couched in positive terms. Christianity is strongest when it is represented by love in action.

Parting Thoughts:
Live for something, have a purpose,
 And that purpose keep in view;
Drifting like a helpless vessel
 Thou canst to life ne'er be true.
Half the wrecks that strew life's ocean,
 If some star had been their guide,
Might have been safely riding,
 But they drifted with the tide.
(Author unknown)

64

15

What Do You Expect Your Religion To Do?

Instrumental Meditation *(The people reverently quiet)*

Words Of Preparation:
The English clergyman and novelist, Charles Kingsley, is reported to have said, "What I want is not to possess religion but to have a religion that shall possess me."

Samuel M. Shoemaker said, "Religion which is merely ritual and ceremonial can never satisfy. Neither can we be satisfied by a religion which is merely humanitarian or serviceable to mankind. Man's craving is for the spiritual."

Hymn: "Mid All The Traffic Of The Ways"

A Prayer Of Invocation:
O Lord, purify our hearts and open our lips, that we may magnify your holy name. Help us to be truly reverent in thought, word and deed in all our living. We seek to worship you now and always in the faith and spirit of Jesus Christ our Lord. Amen.

Scripture: James 1:19-27
You must understand this, my beloved: let everyone be quick to listen, slow to speak, slow to anger; for your anger

does not produce God's righteousness. Therefore rid yourselves of all sordidness and rank growth of wickedness, and welcome with meekness the implanted word that has the power to save your souls.

But be doers of the word, and not merely hearers who deceive themselves. For if any are hearers of the word and not doers, they are like those who look at themselves in a mirror; for they look at themselves and, on going away, immediately forget what they were like. But those who look into the perfect law, the law of liberty, and persevere, being not hearers who forget but doers who act — they will be blessed in their doing.

If any think they are religious, and do not bridle their tongues but deceive their hearts, their religion is worthless. Religion that is pure and undefiled before God, the Father, is this: to care for orphans and widows in their distress, and to keep oneself unstained by the world.

Sermon: "What Do You Expect Your Religion To Do?"

Genuine religion is not an abstraction. It is an inter-active relationship between the living God and persons. The Christian religion is interpreted and revealed to mankind through God's Son Jesus the Christ. When people unite in religious belief and action, their religion becomes a living organism in the midst of their lives. In Christianity it becomes the body of Christ, which we know as the church, at work within human society. Thus religion is not inanimate; it becomes an active faith uniting people in a spiritual mission serving in the world.

We should expect our religion to do more than schedule a program of worship services and societal gathering of the faithful. It should be much more than listening to a sermon, taking part in hymn singing, or the saying of prayers, all of which are appropriate and needful. We should expect our religion to affect our lives, to give them spiritual meaning

66

and dynamic force, rich experience with helpful interpretation of what it means to be alive. It should afford us a means of spiritual control over the inner and external forces that influence and motivate people.

Phillip Brooks told a story about some savages who were given a sun dial, in order that by the casting of the sun's light and shadow on it they might know the time of day. So desirous were they to honor and keep it sacred that they built a roof over it. Sometimes people regard their religion as something to be sheltered and used only on the Sabbath. Religion must be utilized continually to be of real help in life. Ours should be an everyday faith and practice.

We should expect our religion to provide us with a wholesome and helpful understanding of God and humanity's relation with him. It should help us to recognize the fatherhood of God and the brotherhood of man. From these concepts we are enabled to develop social consciousness and group responsibilities. This helps us to establish communication and personal interaction between God and man, and man to all mankind.

We should expect our religion to provide us with literacy in faith and the ethical performances of life. The purpose of religious education is to interpret God and his Word in the provision of a dependable pattern of life, not so much as chapter and verse transmission, as by principle and truth. The goal is to help us all to truly know our God and Christ as Lord, not only by reading and interpretative conversation, but also personally, and in redemptiveness that assures salvation.

We want to know that our religion provides the means for the salvation of our souls. We need to be aware that it is not the church that saves us, but that it offers the prescription for salvation, and the nurture that our souls require for the abundant life. Our salvation is by faith in God through Jesus Christ his Son our Lord. We are saved not from lostness and wrath alone, but to inclusion and purposefulness.

We should expect our religion to establish a dependable ground of theology. We all need a systematic pattern of believing and understanding for the satisfaction of our minds, and the assurance that what we think and do are in keeping with the will and love of God. We need to know that genuine truth and reason undergirds the faith and aspirations of our lives.

Our relation to our religion may be likened unto Jesus' story about those who had worked all day in the fields, and then were directed to prepare and serve the evening meal. (Luke 17) We never quite seem to get everything done that we desire — there is continually something beyond. And that is good. That something else is life eternal!

A Closing Prayer:

O God, grant that we should be faithful in our religious affiliation, and in the performance of life in the ethical, moral, and spiritual manner that God intended, and that Jesus taught. Help us to realize that religion is a very personal thing — a vital relationship between you and us — and that it has its strength in the body of Christ, the church at work in the world. Make us diligent disciples, Lord, ever more interested in serving and preserving the heritage that means the most to all of us — our faith and liberty in truth and love, in the name of Jesus Christ. Amen.

16
Elements Of Devotion

Instrumental Meditation

Words Of Preparation: from The English Bishop, Jeremy Taylor)
"The private devotions and secret offices of religion are like the refreshing of a garden with the distilling and petty drops of a water-pot; but addressed from the temple, they are like rain from heaven."

Hymn: "Sweet Hour Of Prayer"

A Prayer:
O hearts, minds, and souls, be still, that we may hear the soft whispers of God's voice speaking to us amid the rush of life, and the turbulence of our times. Father, speak to us words that we need to hear. We wait for your divine guidance for our lives, for your answers to our problems, pains, and inward distress. In these moments of quiet contemplation, fill our souls with your Spirit. Enable us to dream dreams, see visions, and become obedient to your will and way for our lives, in Jesus' name. Amen.

Scripture: Acts 17:22-28 (NRSV)
Then Paul stood in front of the Areopagus and said, "Athenians, I see how extremely religious you are in every way.

For as I went through the city and looked carefully at the objects of your worship, I found among them an altar with the inscription, 'To an unknown god.' What therefore you worship as unknown, this I proclaim to you. The God who made the world and everything in it, he is Lord of heaven and earth, does not live in shrines made by human hands, nor is he served by human hands, as though he needed anything, since he himself gives to all mortals life and breath and all things. From one ancestor he made all nations to inhabit the whole earth, and he allotted the times of their existence and boundaries of the places where they would live, so that they would search for God and perhaps grope for him and find him — though indeed he is not far from each one of us. For in him we live and move and have our being: as even some of your own poets have said, 'For we too are his offspring.' ''

Sermon: "Elements Of Devotion"

It is a natural urge within man that he find that which is higher than himself to which he may ascribe allegiance, and express devotion. Sometimes these feelings of devotional kind were marked by setting up stones as altars of remembrance, to which return was occasionally made. Sacrifices were offered. Codes for creative and moral living were established. Doing what is right before God as a part of human devotion became the rule of life. Home altars, symbols of faith and experience, and eventually temples and churches were built including altars and symbols of the history of the faith were erected.

Paul noticed an altar with its inscription, "To an unknown god," and decided to help his hearers discover what it was they really wanted: a God whom they could worship in truth and in Spirit. He explained to them that their desire to express devotion was natural, as they, like others, "would search for God and perhaps grope for him and find him — though he indeed is not far from each one of us. For 'in him we live and move and have our being.' ''

70

Devotion means the development of a reverent attitude, accompanied by loyalty and service. The expression of that feeling of devotion may take the form we call devotional, making use of thoughts and prayers. Sometimes the scriptures are read, a guide or manual to aid in the devotional, is utilized, and prayers are read or offered from the heart, and may be expressed privately or in groups. In order to deepen the atmosphere of spiritual devotion, many people have Bibles, crosses or crucifixes, or pictures of artists' concepts of the Christ in their homes, as reminders of what they believe and feel in relation to God. There is also the devotion that is self-giving, expressing itself in filial love, acts of kindness and goodness, and unswerving responsibility.

Within all of us there is the spiritual urge to love and to be loved by God and people. Knowing that we are loved is one of the essentials to happiness and the drive to be creative. People want to be appreciated as being both attractive and lovable personalities, approved of by God and others. Expressed devotions increase the feelings of being adequate and secure.

The desire for goodness in life, and for a wholesome feeling of inner well being, causes us to be devout in our prayers, personal attitude adjustments, and search for ample faith. The individual, family, or group devotions give us feelings of increased faith and spiritual strength.

There is a connection between learned discipline, appropriate behavior, insight, and devotional life. A grandmother told the story of how her three-and-a-half-year-old grandson was a curious and mischievous child. One day he discovered the large crock in which she kept flour behind a lower cabinet door. He was missed and a search began for him. When the grandmother went into the kitchen, she noticed little white puffs coming from under the cabinet door. He had climbed into the flour crock, pulled the door shut, and was enjoying taking a flour bath! The grandmother lifted him out, toweled him off, and then, seeking to teach him a lesson, held his hand in her palm, and lightly spanked it, saying, "Naughty, naughty; you must not do such things!" He then ran through the house, looking for something else interesting to get into, and rubbing his hand, saying, "Naughty hand! Naughty hand!" blaming his hand but not his thinking. As his grandfather was offering the next meal blessing, he was seen rubbing his hand, and whispering, "Naughty! Naughty!" He understood the meaning of the blessing, and that he ought to have been disciplined and corrected. Devotions help in bringing a sense of correctness, even to the very young, as well as to older persons.

There is a sense of power satisfaction that comes through spiritual communion with God. A person may often feel after a devotional experience that the seemingly impossible can now be accomplished.

All of these combined factors help us to realize that there is real purpose in living, and that objectivity and personal wholesomeness are needful for completion of the devotional attitude and accomplishment of a cause.

The Benediction:
O God, as we leave these moments of devotions together, grant that we may have a sense of your abiding presence, courage to face all that is required of us, and that we may accomplish that which is most helpful by the increase of our faith and personal devotion to doing your will. Grant, O Lord, that we shall remember that "in you we live and move and have our being." Amen.

17
The Best Surprises

Instrumental Meditation

A Hymn: "Sometimes A Little Surprises"
(Let the hymn be played through as meditation music, after which the lyrics may be either sung or read.)

Scripture: Matthew 2:9-12 and 4:9-11 (NRSV)
When they had heard the king, they set out; and there ahead of them went the star that they had seen at its rising, until it stopped over the place where the child was. When they saw that the star had stopped, they were overwhelmed with joy. On entering the house they knelt down and paid him homage. Then opening their treasure chests, they offered him gifts of gold, frankincense, and myrrh. And having been warned in a dream not to return to Herod, they left for their own country by another road.

Jesus said, "Is there anyone among you who, if your child asks for bread, will give him a stone? Or if the child asks for a fish, will give him a snake? If you then, being evil, know how to give good gifts to your children, how much more will your father in heaven give good things to those who ask him!"

A Prayer:
O God our Father, we are overwhelmed by the wonderful surprises that you have given unto us. When we behold the

earth, its beauty and bounty, we are amazed. You have surprised us by giving us your Son who became our Teacher and our Savior, making life more meaningful and blessed with his saving grace. Just as the shepherds in the field were surprised when the angels sang of the Lord's birth, and so were Mary and Joseph, when the wise men brought wonderful gifts for the Christ Child, so we are continually amazed at all the blessings and wonders you give us each day of our lives. Thank you for surprising us with the light of salvation, and the promise of goodwill and peace among all men. We hope to surprise and gratify you and ourselves by living the kind of lives that will be a blessing in your kingdom, in the name of Jesus Christ our Lord. Amen.

Hymn: "This Is My Father's World"

Sermon: "The Best Surprises"

Most good things in life are accompanied by anticipation, and even direct preparation, but some are spontaneous surprises, and are extra joys in life.

Some of them are simple joys, like making a new and good friend; renewing old acquaintances without expecting to see them; coming upon the smell of new-mown hay; finding something that you thought had been forever lost; the warm and joyous experience of a new-found relationship with God; the awareness of spiritual assurance after a crisis in life, the lingering joy of great music heard by the ear and felt by the heart.

Other surprises of beauty and wonder come by reason of natural order. Such is the cry of a newborn baby; the thorny bush that bears a beautiful rose with fine aroma; being sound asleep and awakening to the smell of fresh coffee and sizzling bacon; the surprise birthday cake and party; the gift of a wonderful anniversary celebration! It's a great feeling when you are granted a date with a lovely young lady, who also considers you to be the nicest young man in town; when that young man after a wonderful courtship, proposes marriage. There is the time when after diligent study you are told that you are the class valedictorian, and are the recipient of a much-desired college scholarship to the university of your choice. There comes the joy of receiving the job you most wanted, and promotions in the vocation of your choice.

Surprises come in many wonderful ways!

The Messianic prophecy and anticipation had long been expected, but it came in ways that were not. There was a babe born in a borrowed manger; a young adult who taught moderation in preference to militance; one who was willing to die for the sake of atonement for sin and the salvation of humankind — and who would forgive even as he was being killed!

They looked for a vibrant, dynamic personality, not for a soft-spoken, love-teaching, morality-conscious and redemptive-minded Son of God, who would say, "The Father and I are one," and, "No man comes to the Father but by me."

So often we look in the wrong direction, at the wrong person, in the wrong place, for what we ought to be and know we need to be finding in life. It is easy to substitute the ideas of secular success for the higher choice of spiritual grace and service. Values and goals are devalued because we are so engrossed with the details of living, to the end that our home becomes a house, our marriage a convenience instead of an on-going courtship, our work a job instead of a calling filled with vocational pride, our souls barren, and our zest for life chilled. Even John, the cousin and presenter of Jesus became disillusioned, and hearing about the deeds of Jesus, inquired, "Are you the one to come, or shall we look for another?"

Those who have been diligently engaged in the pursuit and fulfillment of the Christian life have been, and continue to be wonderfully surprised. It was like that for the lad who presented Jesus with his small loaves and fishes; and for the man who lay paralyzed, found himself a forgiven man, and took up his pallet and walked home; for Mary Magdalene, who found herself free of inner turmoil, and became the first to see Jesus alive in the garden; and for those who followed Jesus' instructions to remain gathered in Jerusalem, and experienced the Pentecost.

Among our greatest pleasures is surprising others with gifts and joys of life, shared in love and fellowship, and in extended meaningfulness. Such is the case when one convert can help to make another; when one disciple can lead another into total commitment; when the church so gives itself that life becomes a fellowship of faith and triumph in human-spiritual rejoicing. "Sometimes a light surprises the Christian!"

Often we seem surprised when God fulfills his promises — perhaps because we are so prone to forget our own vows, and choose the easy road instead of the rough path. The best surprises may not come in the form or packaging we expect, yet God surprises us with them in "mysterious ways, his wonders to perform." There is a spiritual song that says, "It is no secret what God can do." The greatest joy is what God does through Christ in us. The transformation of life is a wonderful surprise, a grand experience when one gives himself or herself to Christ our Lord, and to the service of his kingdom on earth. There is no greater joy in all of life. We are never too old to make such a decision, and our Lord's invitation is to whosoever will.

A Closing Prayer:

Thank you God, for all your wonderful surprises to the gracious benefit of our lives, especially for the gift of your Son Jesus Christ. Continue, O Lord, to surprise us in those wonderful ways that only you can do. Grant that we may so live, that when our lives come to an earthly conclusion, we may enter into the joy and surprises of life eternal. In Jesus' name. Amen.

18
The Wonderful Mystery Of The Christian Religion

Instrumental Meditation

The Call To Worship:
Since we have a great high priest who has passed through the heavens, Jesus the Son of God, let us with confidence draw near to the throne of grace, that we may receive mercy and find grace to help in time of need.

Come, walk in the way of the Lord with songs of gladness and joy. Amen.

Hymn: "My Savior's Love"

Scripture: 1 Timothy 3:14-16 (NRSV)
I hope to come to you soon, but I am writing these instructions to you so that, if I am delayed, you may know how one ought to behave in the household of God, which is the church of the living God, the pillar and bulwark of the truth. Without any doubt, the mystery of our religion is great:

He was revealed in the flesh,
vindicated in the spirit,
seen by angels,
proclaimed among Gentiles,
believed in throughout the
world,
taken up into glory.

A Prayer:

It is a mystery, O God, how you could love the world so much as to give your only Son, that we, believing in him, might have eternal life, and how he could so compassionately unite with you in becoming atonement for our sins, and rise from the grave, assuring us of the reality of life after death, and proving the estate of life eternal. We give thanks unto you, our Father, and to your Son our Lord, for caring so much for our lives and our souls, as to teach us the way, the truth and the life, and then suffer for our sakes in order that we might be spiritually whole. Grant that we shall so live as to be worthy of your great love and the faith by which we are blessed in this world. In the consciousness of all that is holy, we humbly pray. Amen.

Sermon: "The Wonderful Mystery Of The Christian Religion"

Paul declared, "Without any doubt the mystery of our religion is great," and we find ourselves in agreement for there is no other religion like it. Its wonderful mystery is based on the life and love of Jesus Christ, who became the Savior and Lord of life.

Jesus was the perfect revealer of the nature of God and his concern for mankind. He showed himself as a human being, and met as such, every demand of the Spirit. Without the dynamic of his life in all its aspects, such a redemptive faith could not have come into being.

It is essential that we not only discover the divine mystery of our Lord, and the reasons for our faith in him, but that we also learn how to apply the divine ethic of his life in our own.

What Christianity Means to Me was written by Lynn Abbott when he was 85 years of age. In that work he reported, "It was not until I was about 18 years of age when I came under the influence of Henry Ward Beecher's preaching that I began to understand that Jesus was not a lawgiver, but a

78

lifegiver, and that one is not a Christian because he obeys the laws of God, but he obeys the laws of God because he is a Christian.'' We need to remember that Christianity is not obedience for the sake of legalism, but is righteousness born of redemptive love, and that love centers in Jesus Christ. That is the secret and sweet mystery of this religion.

Christians should not be good for the sake of reward or for the fear of punishment, but because they want to be comfortable with the whole of life, and to enjoy it with the confidence that all is well with our souls.

Douglas Steere wrote *Prayer and Worship* in which he told the story of an old woman who was seen coming along the streets of Strasbourg. She was carrying a pail of water in one hand and a torch in the other. When asked why she was carrying these things, she answered that with the pail of water she was going to put out the flames of hell, and with the torch she was going to burn up heaven, so that in the future people could love the dear Lord God for himself alone, and not out fear of hell, or for the craving for the reward of heaven. Her method and her means may not have been adequate, but her philosophy was excellent.

A part of the great mystery of our religion is the knowledge that ''God is love,'' (1 John 4:8) and that ''God so loved the world that he gave his only Son that whoever believes in him should not perish but have eternal life.'' (John 3:16)

This little poem, the author of which is unknown, speaks a profound truth.

> *A weathercock that once was placed*
> *A farmer's barn above,*
> *Bore on it by its owner's will,*
> *The sentence, "God is love."*
>
> *His neighbor passing questioned him;*
> *he deemed his legend strange —*
> *"How dost thou think, that like the vane,*
> *God's love can lightly change?"*

The farmer, smiling, shook his head.
"Nay, friend, 'tis meant to show
That 'God is love' which ever way
The wind may chance to blow."

It is true; no matter which way the winds may blow, Jesus Christ is the same, yesterday, today, and tomorrow, and God's love remains constant. That also is part of the wonderful mystery of the Christian faith.

The hymn that we often sing in parting, "God Be With You Till We Meet Again," illustrates our confidence in the wonderful mystery of the Christian religion. Its author, Jeremiah Eames Rankin, told this story of its origin.

"Written in 1882 as a Christian's goodbye, it was called forth by no person or occasion, but was deliberately composed as a Christian hymn on the basis of the etymology of 'goodbye,' which is 'God be with you.' It was set to music composed by William Gould Tomer, and was first sung in the First Congregational Church, Washington, D.C., where Rev. Rankin was the pastor. It was much used by the Christian Endeavor, a youth organization. It became a favorite of British soldiers during the South African War, as it appeared in the Sankey book of hymns, No. 494. That is why 494 became the military secret password. After more than a century it is still a favorite and a comfort to many.

Let us leave this service with the text of today's message lingering in our minds: "Without any doubt, the mystery of our religion is great."

Hymn: "God Be With You"

80

19
For Goodness Sake

Instrumental Meditation

Something Worth Thinking About:
There is so much good in the worst of us,
And so much bad in the best of us,
That it ill behooves any of us
To find fault with the rest of us.
— Anonymous

Abhor that which is evil; cleave to that which is good . . . .
Be not overcome of evil, but overcome evil with good.
— Romans 12:9, 21

The heart of a good man is the sanctuary of God.
— Madame Anne Germaine de Stael

Hymn: "I Would Be True"

Scripture: Mark 10:17-22 (NRSV)
As he was setting out on a journey, a man ran up and knelt before him, and asked him, "Good Teacher, what must I do to inherit eternal life?" Jesus said to him, "Why do you call me good? No one is good but God alone. You know the commandments: 'You shall not murder; You shall not commit adultery; You shall not steal; You shall not bear false witness; You shall not defraud; Honor your father and mother.' "

He said to him, "Teacher, I have kept all these since my youth." Jesus, looking at him, loved him and said, "You lack one thing; go sell what you own, and give the money to the poor, and you will have treasure in heaven; then come follow me." When he heard this he was shocked and went away grieving, for he had many possessions.

A Prayer:

O good and gracious God, open our minds and our hearts that we may fully receive the message of this portion of the gospel, and the truth as your Son Jesus sought to impart it. Enhance our ability to discern goodness, to admire it, to aspire to it, and to be faithful in trying to be true to the principles that make for goodness in all things. Amen.

———————

Sermon: "For Goodness Sake"

Mildred and Jessie were sisters, very dear and close throughout their more than 80 years of life. They had a common expression which each of them used often, when they were excited, surprised, vexed, or undecided: "Oh, for goodness sake," or simply "For goodness sake!" The tone of voice or emphasis given, demonstrated their feelings. Neither of them ever used swear words. The phrase, "For goodness sake!" was sufficient emphasis for each of them. Each of them married, had families, and contributed a great deal of goodness to life. It seemed that they lived for goodness sake, and they were admired for it.

Many years ago Harvey Branscomb wrote a book titled, *The Teachings Of Jesus,* in which he said, "Goodness of character is not so many deeds, be they ever so valuable. It is an ongoing process of the soul. It does not mean character that is fixed, hardened into a mold, but life that is ever growing and reshaping itself to higher ends."

Students of the English language know that there are four degrees of goodness: good, better, best, and perfect. Jesus taught, "Be perfect, therefore, as your heavenly Father is perfect." (Matthew 5:48)

In this situation Jesus was upholding the perfectness of God. Jesus seemed to understand himself as being both human and divine, since he knew that he was the Son of God, but he did not feel that his humanness before this man entitled him to be called good in the sense it applied to God the Father. Paul Scherer said of this: "Only God is entitled to the absolute predicate good."

Matthew's gospel phrases Jesus' question a bit differently than does Mark and Luke, to read, "Why do you ask me about what is good?" In this story there arises the matter of sinlessness of both the inquirer and Jesus. The response of Jesus points to obedience to the Law as the primary requirement for human goodness. The seeker feels that though he has been obedient, something is still missing, so he asks, "What else is necessary?" The answer is, "Total commitment." Jesus was aware, even as he gave counsel, that he too must come to terms with total commitment, which would not be easy, and may very well cost him the penalty of death. Giving what you have may be difficult, but giving your life for the sake of others is the ultimate goodness.

We sometimes think of goodness in terms of abilities and qualifications. Talent and learning combined make us more able, which is a form of goodness. High standards of morality in concept and performance cause us to be known as good. Genuine spirituality lived to the best of one's capacity as a person adds to goodness of the soul of the individual and those whom he or she touches. The highest good is that which enriches this life and assures eternal life.

It is important that we, as Christians, remember that goodness alone is not enough. We must also be justified by faith, through our Lord Jesus Christ. Morality and pure performance are not enough. The basics of faith go deeper than simply being good. We must give ourselves away to the will and purpose of God.

Henry Thoreau said, "Be not merely good; be good for something." That was Jesus' challenge to the man who wanted to know what he could do to inherit eternal life. He had been good at making money, in being morally upright and keeping the commandments; but that is not the ultimate good: he must also give of himself and what he has in behalf of others. He needed to also realize that, "The gift without the giver is bare."

John Wesley proposed an excellent guide to goodness. He said, and he practiced what he preached:

Do all the good you can,
By all the means you can,
In all the ways you can,
At all the times you can,
As long as ever you can.

Someone else has expressed the ideal of goodness in a wonderful way, saying, "I expect to pass through this world but once; any good thing therefore, that I can do, or any goodness that I can show to my fellow creatures, let me do it now; let me not defer or neglect it, for I shall not pass this way again."

Paul wrote, "Test everything; hold fast to what is good; abstain from every form of evil." (1 Thessalonians 5:21)

———————

Hymn: "Dear Master, In Whose Life I See"
(May be either sung or read as a closing prayer.)

20
When The Heart Is Right Before God

Instrumental Meditation

Words Of Preparation: Psalm 51:10-12 (NRSV)
Create in me a clean heart, O God,
    and put a right spirit within me.
Do not cast me away from your presence,
    and do not take your holy spirit from me.
Restore to me the joy of your salvation,
    and sustain in me a willing spirit. Amen.

Hymn: "Near To The Heart Of God"

Scripture: Acts 8:9-24 (NRSV)
Now a certain man, named Simon had previously practiced magic in the city and amazed the people of Samaria, saying that he was someone great. All of them, from the least to the greatest, listened to him eagerly, saying, "This man is the power of God that is called Great." And they listened eagerly to him because for a long time he had amazed them with his magic. But when they believed Philip, who was proclaiming the good news about the kingdom of God and the name of Jesus Christ, they were baptized, both men and women. Even Simon himself believed. After being baptized, he stayed constantly with Philip and was amazed when he saw the signs and great miracles that took place.

Now when the apostles at Jerusalem heard that Samaria had accepted the word of God, they sent Peter and John to them. The two went down and prayed for them that they might receive the Holy Spirit (for as yet the Spirit had not come upon any of them; they had only been baptized in the name of the Lord Jesus). Then Peter and John laid their hands on them, and they received the Holy Spirit. Now when Simon saw that the Spirit was given through the laying on of the apostles' hands, he offered them money, saying, "Give me also this power so that anyone on whom I lay my hands may receive the Holy Spirit." But Peter said to him, "May your silver perish with you, because you thought you could obtain God's gift with money! You have no part or share in this for your heart is not right before God. Repent therefore of this wickedness of yours, and pray to the Lord that, if possible, the intent of your heart may be forgiven you. For I see that you are in the gall of bitterness and the chains of wickedness." Simon answered, "Pray for me to the Lord, that nothing of what you have said may happen to me."

Sermon: "When The Heart Is Right Before God"

In the Revised Standard Version, the notation is made that Psalm 51 is a prayer offered by David after Nathan the prophet had rebuked him for his illicit relationship with Bathsheba. David also caused the death of Uriah whom he ordered put in the front lines of battle. He knew that his heart was not right with God, nor was he just in his human decisions.

The story from Acts 8 has to do with selfish and mistaken motives on the part of the new covenant, Simon, and ends with his being truly contrite, and asking for help from the apostles.

Thinking, doing, and feeling right is of vital concern to all conscientious persons. Impulsiveness and personal ambition often get ordinarily good people into difficulty. David wanted and took that which was not right or honorable, including another man's wife and his life. Simon misunderstood

86

the wonderful mystery of the faith, and thought that money might be the answer to getting the special power that he did not have. His motivation was seriously wrong.

All of us, in any aspect of life, may get our priorities confused, and may do that which is not right because of our refusal to consider the true issues of morality and responsibility. Sometimes people get the idea that older people don't have such problems! Let us beware. We never become so old that temptation cannot assail us. For instance, it is easy for us, in the name of senior years to get the idea that because we are older we are to be better served, and that special privilege ought always to be ours, so we are tempted to make demands that we should not, and are hard on other people. Because we are senior persons doesn't make our taking advantage of someone right. Something is only right when it is not wrong.

Everything needs to stand on its own merits, rather than upon the desire of some person, or the pressure of some group. Not everything that seems desirable at a given moment may ultimately be the right thing to do. Time, understanding, and evaluation temper many things. Patience and serious consideration are needful in making correct judgments. It is much harder to undo a wrong than to do right in the first place. In deciding for the right, several criteria should be utilized. The following are here suggested.

•Is this decision fair to all who may be concerned?

•Am I being completely honest with myself and with others?

•Is this prudent in practice, and will the result be fruitful or helpful?

•Am I being theologically correct, and will it stand the test of what God expects of us?

•Will my decision and action be spiritually uplifting, or will it lower my standards and leave me with a sense of being less than pure, or at my best?

•Though it may seem right for me, will what I decide hurt anyone else?

William Jennings Bryan once said something well worth our hearing again, for it is excellent counsel.

"Never be afraid to stand with the minority when the minority is right, for the minority will one day be the majority; always be afraid to stand with the majority which is wrong, for the majority which is wrong will one day be the minority."

If we believe in the goodness of God and the ultimate triumph of righteousness, then we may feel spiritually secure in the present, and fully confident of the future. When the heart is right before God, we have no reason to fear anything else, for what really matters in this life is knowing all is well with our souls, and God approves.

Hymn: "It Is Well With My Soul"

The Closing Prayer:
O God, send down upon us your Holy Spirit, to cleanse our hearts and hallow our lives. Grant your mercy to us, and bestow upon us your grace and salvation. Accompany us with your divine presence, encouraging us to live in peace, love, and holiness; through Jesus Christ our Lord. Amen.

21
A Larger Design For Living

Instrumental Meditation *(The people quietly prayerful)*

Words Of Preparation from 1 Peter 2:4-5
Come to him, a living stone, though rejected by mortals yet chosen and precious in God's sight, and like living stones, let yourselves be built into a spiritual house.

Hymn: "Higher Ground"

Scripture: Matthew 7:24-29 (NRSV)
Jesus said, "Everyone who hears these words of mine and acts on them will be like a wise man who built his house on a rock. The rain fell, the floods came, and the winds blew and beat on that house, but it did not fall, because it had been founded on a rock. And everyone who hears these words of mine and does not act on them will be like a foolish man who built his house on sand. The rain fell, and floods came, and the winds blew and beat against that house, and it fell — and great was its fall!"
Now when Jesus had finished saying these things, the crowds were astonished at his teaching, for he taught them as one having authority, and not as their scribes.

A Brief Prayer:
O God, we desire that our ears, hearts, and minds shall be fully receptive to the words of our Lord Jesus Christ. Add unto us the ability to think clearly, to reason well, and to make

good decisions in life, not only by means of learning, but also by insight and the guidance of your Holy Spirit. Grant unto us that we may discover and utilize the larger design for living as creative and strong Christians in your kingdom on earth and in heaven. Amen.

Sermon: "A Larger Design For Living"

When Burl G. Kreps was pastor of Good Shepherd Church in Security, Colorado, he wrote an article that appeared in the May, 1973 issue of *Circuit Rider*, titled, "Keeping the Right Perspective." In it he said, "Each one of us needs to search his own conscience and realize there is a larger design for living. Then we can stop making excuses and be one with God's purposes." That phrase triggered the title for this message.

People sometimes have a limited view of life, which is often self-imposed. There are those who hesitate to be concerned about it because they prefer not to be responsible for what they might discover. There are those who feel it is easier to plod along like a work horse wearing a blind sided bridle, so as not to be distracted.

Great living requires a larger view of life than our own self interests. There are times when we may have been prone to stifle conscience and look the other way to avoid harsh reality and the part we ought to play in the drama of life. It has been noted that some people resent necessitous change so much that they will pretend that they are 39 for as long as they can.

You may recall that Robert Louis Stevenson, the poet, was a very unwell man. As he was approaching the latter days of his life, a clergyman sent him a message, saying that he would be glad to visit and talk with him "as one in danger of dying." Stevenson replied with a note that said he didn't want him to come to talk with him "as one in danger of dying," but he would be glad to see him and talk with him "as one in danger of living." Stevenson believed in the larger design of living.

In the early pages of his book, *Fortitude,* Hugh Walpole wrote, "'Tisn't life that matters! 'Tis the courage you bring to it!'' Yes, it takes courage not to go along with the crowd and popular opinion, or to stand tall for what you believe is right, regardless of the cost. It took tremendous courage for the Lord when he was raised up on the cross to cry out, ''Father, forgive them, for they know not what they do.''

We need to live as those who constantly desire to rise above the low planes of crassness, immoral indulgence, and unethical practices. It is our essential obligation to seek to be better today and tomorrow than we were yesterday in every arena of our lives. Goodness is not merely abstention from evil, which is not enough. Goodness that leads to the greater good for ourselves and for others is goodness in action. That is the way to put the larger design for living into meaningful service.

Also essential to the larger design for living is having a vision of a greater tomorrow. We cannot live by the code of doom and gloom if we are to have a brighter and better tomorrow. We need to get busy preventing the conditions that breed failure, sadness, brokenness, and confusion. We need to exhibit the confidence that rightness triumphs, and that faith grows in spite of adversity. It is our business to inspire by what we believe, and to become transformers instead of conformers. Paul wrote to Timothy, ''God did not give us a spirit of cowardice, but rather a spirit of power and love and of self-discipline.'' (2 Timothy 1:7) Christians are not supposed to be controlled by life; they should control life! We sometimes have too small a vision of what God expects of us.

Michaelangelo came one day into the studio of Rafael and was looking at one of Rafael's early drawings. Then he took a piece of chalk and wrote across the drawing, ''Amplius,'' which means ''greater, and larger.'' Rafael's ideas had been too cramped and narrow. Like the great master artist, God sometimes looks on our design for living, and leaves us with the word, ''Amplius.'' And in the same way that Rafael became a greater artist on canvas, so we ought to develop a larger design for our lives in keeping with the inspiration of God and his directions for them. We need a greater comprehension of what God expects of us in carrying out the design for living. There are several things we need to remember.

"A man's life does not consist in the abundance of his possessions." (Luke 12:15)

"Life is more than food, and the body more than clothing." (Luke 12:23)

"He that findeth his life shall lose it, and he that loseth his life shall find it." (Matthew 10:39)

It is needful for us to realize that our lives must be self-disciplined, guided by God, and that we should defer to the wealth of experience that causes us to review and enlarge our design for living. All of us need a measure of authority in our lives, and all of us will do well to understand that being a good servant may be the highest honor which we may attain. Only a few can be chiefs; most must be braves.

There are some lyrics that begin with, "Build thee more stately mansions, O my soul; leave thy low-vaulted past." This is a wonderful reminder of what we mean when we talk about a larger design for living. We should all, regardless of circumstances, aspire to a larger design for living, and an ever enriching perspective of life. An architect once said to a building committee, "It is not possible to properly design a building unless you know why and how you want it to serve." Purpose should ever be in our minds as we plan ahead for victorious living, and eternal joy.

A Closing Prayer:

O God, we know that you care about all of us, no matter how old we become, how limited we may appear to be, or when we lose our courage and our incentive to attempt the difficult things in life. Grant, O Lord, that we shall not let our dreams, our visions, and our hopes dwindle away. Enable us to share them with those who come after us, so that if we should not be able to complete what you have put into our minds and hearts within the days of our years, they shall yet be put into effect in due time because they are truly worth the effort. This we humbly ask in Jesus' name, because we believe in a larger design for living. Amen.

22
Vitality
For Today

Meditation Music: "God Of Grace And God Of Glory"
(May be sung as a solo to emphasize its message)

Words Of Encouragement from Philippians 3:13-15
Paul wrote: "This one thing I do: forgetting what lies behind and straining forward to what lies ahead, I press on toward the goal for the prize of the heavenly call of God in Christ Jesus. Let those of us then who are mature be of the same mind; and if you think differently about anything, this too God will reveal to you. Only let us hold fast to what we have attained."

A Prayer:
Gracious and loving God, we, as your children, have come here to worship, to seek encouragement for living our days to their fullest, and to dedicate ourselves anew to living vital and meaningful lives. Enable us to rise above our worries and fears, to look forward to your daily blessings, and to the joy of having a part in the kingdom of heaven. In Jesus' name we pray. Amen.

Hymn: "Just When I Need Him Most"

Scripture: 2 Corinthians 4:16-18 (NRSV)
We do not lose heart. Even though our outer nature is wasting away, our inner nature is being renewed day by day. For

this slight momentary affliction is preparing us for an eternal weight of glory beyond all measure, because we look not at what can be seen, but at what cannot be seen: for what can be seen is temporary, but what cannot be seen is eternal.

Sermon: "Vitality For Today"

What a wonderful thought! "Even though our outer nature is wasting away, our inner nature is being renewed day by day." There are a considerable number of people, who, though in their 90s, are still living vital, lively, and creative lives. Those who see Willard Scott on television, are privileged each day to get a glimpse of numerous people celebrating life for a hundred and more years, some of them still active in the use of their talents and wisdom. The important thing is don't lose heart — remain vital in your thinking and activities.

Healthy attitude is essential to meaningful life in every circumstance of our being. Inner desire is necessary for playing the game of life well. It is especially valuable when we need to perform under conditions of physical limitations.

It is a wonderful thing to know that God adds vitality to our lives by the presence of his Spirit within us! All of us need to be aware of something extra by which to live, and to increase meaningfulness in the midst of our daily experiences. Vitality for today is urgent for all of us.

It has been generally understood that human life matures in seven-year cycles. This is reasonably true for most of us, with some variation. At about age 35 we begin to notice that we are experiencing some noticeable changes in physical performance, and that many of the things that mattered in youth and early adulthood are less important now. We begin to consider the needful economies of life, including provision for the later years of our lives. Personal maturity, spiritual fitness, and summary achievement begin to take on new meanings for us. We may even begin to consider what people will think and say of us when we have arrived at retirement, or finished our course of life.

It is important that each and all of us, as we grow older, make sure that our inner nature is being renewed every day. Concern for things that endure is essential to our well-being. It is good for each of us to ask himself or herself, "If this were the last day of my life, would I know that all is well with my soul? Have I intentionally renewed my inner being so that my earthly state matches the nature of life eternal?"

It is so easy for us to take life for granted, to let things slide along, and to put off that which ultimately matters most.

Daily renewal of the spiritual self prepares us to face the factors of life with confidence. It also prepares us to deal with the unexpected, the critical moments, and the undesired conditions in which we may find ourselves involved.

It is needful that we regularly or frequently pray, establishing continual communication with God as our Friend as well as our Divine Counselor and Helper. William Hinson, in *A Place to Dig*, has said, "Prayer is not productive of some kind of magical power. Prayer is like the rudder on the end of the windmill. It keeps us open to the power that comes from God through the Spirit who wills to dwell within us."

Because we practice spiritual disciplines, a devout relationship with God, and a loving relationship with our fellow-beings, does not assure us that we will have no rough places in our lives. It does give us confidence that we will be better able to deal with them. Paul said, "I can do all things through him who strengthens me." (Philippians 4:13)

Our spiritual awareness and knowledge should be increasing by inverse ratio to our physical aging processes, else we are not exercising our natural endowments to accrue wisdom, understanding, and insight in relation to our human experience. There is a measure of truth in the television advertisement that had a lady saying, "I'm not getting older; I'm getting better every day."

We all will do well to remember, "Do not lose heart. Even though our outer nature is wasting away, our inner nature is being renewed day by day." This becomes vitality for today.

An Ascription Of Praise: from 1 Peter 5-11

The God of all grace, who has called you to his eternal glory in Christ, will himself restore, establish, and strengthen you. To him be dominion for ever and ever. Amen.

23

What Are You Doing With The Rest Of Your Life?

Instrumental Meditation

Words Of Preparation: from Psalm 90:1-2, 10, 12 (NRSV)
Lord, you have been our dwelling place in all
generations.
Before the mountains were brought forth, or ever you
had formed the earth and the world, from everlasting
to everlasting you are God.

The days of our life are seventy years, or perhaps
eighty, if we are strong.

So teach us to count our days that we may gain a wise
heart.

Hymn: "O For A Closer Walk With God"

A Prayer:
O God our help in ages past, our hope for years to come,
we are here to consider what we are going to do with the rest
of our lives. Sometimes, Father, we act as if that doesn't really have to be thought about, and we put it off. But we know
it does, for we are responsible before you every moment of
our being. We need to discover how to make our remaining
years and days count for the most and the best. We ask your
guidance in this, so that neither we nor those who come after

us will have cause for shame or disappointment. Stimulate us to think, to plan, and to do with the good of your kingdom in mind, Father. This we humbly pray in Jesus' name. Amen.

Scripture: 1 Peter 4:1-2, 7b-11

Since therefore Christ suffered in the flesh, arm yourselves also with the same intention . . . so as to live for the rest of your earthly life no longer by human desires but by the will of God. . . . Therefore be serious and discipline yourselves for the sake of your prayers. Above all, maintain constant love for one another, for love covers a multitude of sins. Be hospitable to one another without complaining. Like good stewards of the manifold grace of God, serve one another with whatever gift each of you has received. Whoever speaks must do so as one speaking the very words of God; whoever serves must do it with the strength that God supplies, so that God may be glorified in all things through Jesus Christ. To him belong the glory and the power forever and ever. Amen.

Sermon: "What Are You Doing With The Rest Of Your Life?"

In the second verse of 1 Peter 4, these words stand out: "Live for the rest of your life no longer by human desires, but by the will of God." Let us consider that to be the text for this message.

An article appeared in which Norma W. Gaskill referred to two lines from two songs: "What are you doing with the rest of your life?" and "What a difference a day makes." Then she pointed out two important factors: "Time is opportunity," and "Time is a gift." She added, "It is not the amount of time we are allocated, but the use we make of it that is significant." We need to consider the question, "What are you doing with the rest of your life?"

Perhaps we ought to ask a few questions. "How should I plan to use the rest of my life?" "Will I be able to deal with the unexpected or any crises?" "How should I react to what I discover to be the inevitable?"

Let us pretend that it occurs to us that we would do well to prepare a list of things we want to see accomplished in the remainder of our days. What would you put on that list? It might include:

1. Making sure that my heart and soul are right with God, and that I have taken the steps necessary to assure my spiritual salvation.

2. Seek to establish reconciliation between myself and those who may have been hurt in our life relationships.

3. Do that which I have been putting off because it seemed too hard or distasteful to me.

4. Make sure that my temporal affairs are all in order so that no one will be imposed upon because of my neglecting to do so.

If you knew that you had only a week to live, what would you do with each of those seven days? How much time would you waste before attending to necessary matters? How much time would you spend in resting and sleeping? With whom would you most desire to spend those days and final hours? What would you want to make the first priority in your agenda?

Life should not be wasted. We must continually have goals to be met, no matter what our circumstances may be, or how much time we think we may have. In our normal routine of life, we usually expect to utilize in the course of a day, eight hours for vocation, eight hours for leisure and special interests, and eight hours for rest and sleep. The hours may vary for each of these, but a proportional division is needed for good feelings about ourselves and the state of our lives. Without some order and routine we achieve less than we should, especially if we lack suffecient relaxation and sleep.

Visualizing a goal is very necessary. When Florence Chadwick attempted to swim from Catalina to Long Beach, she gave up because of a combination of fog and feeling fatigued. When she had been taken out of the water, and a little later realized how close she was to shore, she said, "I wouldn't have lost if I could have seen my goal." If the swimmer had kept going a little longer, the shoreline would have been revealed through the fog. A little more planning and visualization may also help us to see our goals, and attain them.

We can't afford to allow age to impede our thought and reasoning processes. Older people have a tendency to do that. As we grow older we are likely to think that we have seen it all. When that happens we fail to see new goals, and we lose the essential spark of life needed for accomplishments. It might be said, "We are already dead when we have lost the incentive to improve." The Harvard theologian Harvey Cox, suggested that the greatest sin is shirking responsibility for full actualization of human potential.

Arthur Rubenstein, at age 80, reached greater heights than he had known in his long career. In an interview he was asked how he still kept his interpretations fresh and inspiring. Mr. Rubenstein answered, "Every day I am a new man, and every occasion is a new moment for me. When I play, it is no longer I, but a secret power that takes over."

Life needs to be like that for us and it can be if we will desire and determine it to be so. Our achievements are in direct proportion to our aspirations; seldom are they ever higher than our hopes and dreams. So dream largely, and live fully, blessed by the Spirit of God, and the assurance of things hoped for — this is faith at work in our lives. Let us keep it so!

And "live for the rest of your earthly life no longer by human desires but by the will of God." When we know that we are doing that, the rest will fall into place.

A Closing Prayer:

O God, one of the temptations and sins of old age is giving up, caring no longer, and wishing that we were dead. We can, if we will, do something about the first two things, and we know that we should leave the last one up to you. We

100

know that the important thing is to be properly ready when the last of these things occurs. In the meanwhile, Lord, help us to put as much "spunk" as possible into planning and caring, remembering that so long as we are alive, we are accountable for how we think, say, and do. Help us to avoid becoming pessimists and whiners; instead, help us to become optimists and creative personalities, so that we may prove to be an inspiration to others. These things we pray in the name of Jesus Christ our Lord and Savior. Amen.

The Parting Hymn: "Lord, Dismiss Us With Thy Blessing" *(May be either sung or read as a prayer)*

24

Take Up Your Cross
And Follow Me

Meditation Hymn: "Above The Hills Of Time"
(May be sung as a solo in preparation for worship)

Prayer Of Invocation:
We come to worship you, our Lord, knowing that you overcame both the cross and the grave. We realize that except for your endurance of the cross and its cruel death, we would not have known the full magnitude of your love for us. Your having made atonement for our sins, makes us aware that we should live the Christian faith fully, knowing that it is the way, the truth, and the life. Thank you, Lord, for conquering the cross and winning our hearts and souls for your kingdom. Amen.

Hymn: "The Old Rugged Cross"

Scripture: Matthew 16:24-26 (NRSV)
Then Jesus told his disciples, "If any want to become my followers, let them deny themselves and take up their cross and follow me. For those who want to save their life will lose it, and those who lose their life for my sake will find it. For what will it profit them if they gain the whole world but forfeit their life? Or what will they give in return for their life?"

Sermon: "Take Up Your Cross Daily"

Jesus spoke about the cross on several occasions, because it was to take center stage in the drama of his life, and it was to be remembered by people everywhere in terms of his sacrifice for all souls of all people.

He said, "Whoever does not carry the cross and follow me cannot be my disciple." (Luke 14:27) "If any want to become my followers, let them deny themselves, and take up their cross daily, and follow me." (Luke 9:23) "Whoever does not take up his cross and follow me is not worthy of me." (Matthew 10:38)

Older persons are likely to best remember Matthew 16:24 as found in the King James Version: "For what is a man profited if he shall gain the whole world and lose his own soul? Or what shall a man give in exchange for his soul?"

Certainly, Jesus challenged people to discipleship, when he said, "Take up your cross and follow me." He did not say that the Christian way of life would be easy; rather, he told them that it would be hard, and would require personal sacrifice. He never soft-pedaled the call to discipleship.

The Christian cross is requisite to discipleship. It is a qualification of Christian self-worth. It is more than incidental and occasional; it is a daily matter, and a full-time commitment.

It has to do with ultimate values. Jesus told them that you can only keep what you give away — your life. Selflessness is the only assured means of spiritual survival. He asked them if anything could ever replace it; if they thought they could get it back, once they've let it go. Jesus was telling them that the surest way to keep their souls (lives) was to commit themselves to God's way and will. He warned them that their families and friends might not understand, and that those they loved might turn against them for their decision. Becoming a Christian and taking up the cross was not a thing to be done lightly.

Taking up the cross may mean different things to different people. For some it meant letting go of someone or something precious to them. It could mean giving up something

103

we have wanted in order for someone else to have what is most needed. It may mean responsibility for that which we know our consciences will not allow us to ignore. For the most sincere, it means giving up what we have been doing, and devoting our entire lives to a demanding discipline and fellowship of service and personalized mission, such as the gospel ministry, medicine, teaching, social service, the legal profession, or even statesmanship. For nearly everyone it means going from what we have been (perhaps successfully) to what we ought to be now (even though proportionately less profitable). It boils down to the question, "What does God want me to do now?" It was not a matter of job marketing of skills and benefits, but of what needs to be done now.

We do well to remember that in those days there were no pensions plans, no social security program, or job-related health insurance arrangements. It was not a matter of what does this discipleship pay or do for me, but what can I give and do to make it successful and meaningful to others?

For us in these days, when retirement comes, we may need to take up a new or different cross in life. Nowhere did Jesus say it had to be the same cross every day, but it needs to be our own, taken up with prayer. Christian responsibility is not limited to a single cause or idea. One of the great things about Christianity is that it is filled with so many different and wonderful ideas for expressing love and service to others. Jesus took up his cross to express his love for God and people, and to serve as the personalized atonement for all sin, and to become the means of spiritual redemption for all mankind.

The cross has been said to be the great plus sign for our lives. It means more to our being than just existing. It means carrying a banner that expresses faith, love, and the willingness to sacrifice for what we know ought to be, and is to become reality in our personal and social experiences. It is to serve for the fulfillment of our spiritual lives.

If for a time you have laid down your cross, you can choose to take it up again, or choose another one, perhaps more meaningful, under which to serve, as you feel our Lord directs you to do, and follow him. Be unafraid to ask, "What does God want me to be and do now?" And as you discover the answer, take up your cross and follow him, remembering, "There's a cross for everyone, and there's a cross for me." Yes, there is a cross for every age and state of life.

Hymn: "Take Up Thy Cross"

The Sending Forth:
As we leave this time of worship, let us remember:
"The cross that he gave may be heavy,
But it ne'er outweighs his grace;
The storm that I feared may surround me,
But it ne'er excludes his face.
The cross is not greater than his grace,
The storm cannot hide his blessed face;
I am satisfied to know
That with Jesus here below,
I can conquer every foe."
Go then, bearing your cross in the peace, power and love of the Father, Son and Holy Spirit. Amen.

25
Managing Disappointment

Instrumental Meditation

Words Of Preparation: using words which Jesus quoted while on the cross, from Psalm 22:1-5 (NRSV)
My God, my God, why hast thou forsaken me?
Why are you so far from helping me, from the words
of my groaning?
O my God, I cry by day, but you do not answer; and
by night, but find no rest.
Yet you are holy, enthroned on the praises of Israel.
In you they trusted, and you delivered them.
To you they cried, and were saved; in you they trusted,
and were not put to shame.

Hymn: "What A Friend"

Scripture: Romans 5:1-11 (NRSV)
Therefore, since we are justified by faith, we have peace with God through our Lord Jesus Christ, through whom we have obtained access to his grace in which we stand; and we boast in our hope of sharing the glory of God. And not that only, but we also boast of our sufferings, knowing that suffering produces endurance, and endurance produces character, and character produces hope, and hope does not disappoint us, because God's love has been poured into our hearts through the Holy Spirit that was given to us.

For while we were still weak, at the right time Christ died for the ungodly, Indeed, rarely will anyone die for a righteous person though perhaps for a good person someone might actually dare to die. But God proves his love for us in that while we were yet sinners Christ died for us. Much more surely then, now that we have been justified by his blood, will we be saved through him from the wrath of God. For if while we were enemies, we were reconciled to God through the death of his Son, much more surely having been reconciled, we will be saved by his life. But more than that, we even boast in God through our Lord Jesus Christ, through whom we have now received reconciliation.

A Prayer:

O God our Father, you well know that for the elderly, the frail, the shut-in, the bed-ridden, the nursing or retirement home resident, and hospitalized patients, disappointments are emotionally painful, and cause feelings of having been deserted. Help those we pray, who have such feelings, that they may find relief from their sorrows and disappointments. Cause all who should, to visit, to genuinely care, and to relieve the heartaches of the lonely, the disabled, and the neglected.

Bless, O Lord, the care-givers in all such situations, including family members, friends, nurses, physicians, and ministers, that they shall love and comfort those who experience serious disappointments and feel separation from persons and things they have loved.

These things we humbly ask in the name of our Lord Jesus the Christ. Amen.

Sermon: "Managing Disappointment"

Paul wrote to the Romans, "Endurance produces character, and character produces hope, and hope does not disappoint us, because God's love has been poured into our hearts through the Holy Spirit that has been given to us." (Romans 5:4-5)

Of this we can be sure, even though we feel that God has also forgotten us, he hasn't. Some things are not fully understood until we have felt entirely bereft of all comfort. Disappointment may give us the feeling that no one loves us anymore, and that there is no one who cares. Of this we need to be aware: people are sometimes heavily taxed in their multiple tasks, and because we feel trapped in our situation, we tend to blame them for things they cannot do any better.

Disappointment is common to everyone. It often occurs when least expected, and may become traumatic, leaving the disappointed one with a sense of devastation. The degree of disappointment is in direct proportion to the intensity of anticipation or expectation of an event or a person.

Disappointment can be painful, especially when it involves the emotions of trust and love, and the object of our confidence and affection turns out to have feet of clay. It takes time to recover from intense disappointment, and often requires in-depth evaluation and re-assessment of self and the circumstances and the need for understanding and renewal of self-esteem.

One of the most difficult feelings of disappointment is in the realm of theological factors. If our concept of the who, what, and why of God becomes involved, and we have an inadequate or misinformed idea of his nature and character, we can easily feel that God has let us down, resulting in a diminishment of personal faith, and leading to feelings of agnosticism.

Among the most obvious dangers relating to disappointment is that we may be prone to jump to hasty conclusions, and misjudge the situation that caused the uncomfortable moments.

Another danger is that we may tend to substitute resentment, and even anger for feelings of disappointment, allowing ourselves to become bitter and block out any further feelings of trust in anyone or any social structure. We may even mistrust ourselves both individually and as a collective group.

The appropriate management becomes a necessity for us, else our lives experience disorganization and inner chaos.

Spiritual concepts and values diminish; selfishness rises, and ignoring reality is used as a defense against being hurt again.

We can learn from Jesus. On several occasions he was very disappointed, but he never allowed his disappointment to defeat his purposes in life, or to diminish his belief in the ultimate triumph of righteousness and fulfillment in life.

He was bound to have been disappointed when the rich young ruler, with such great potential, was turned away because his large possessions hampered him.

He was terribly disappointed when Judas Iscariot, one of the original 12 disciples, was found to be an embezzler, then betrayed him for a price; yet he never allowed his disappointment to divert his obligation to become the Savior, or lessen his sense of compassion, even for his betrayer.

He must have been disappointed when all the other 11 disciples fled when he was placed on trial for sedition, and when Peter so vehemently denied him. Yet, after it was over, he sat down with them to discuss the care of the flock, and stood before them to give the great commission. He never gave up on those who seemed to have seriously disappointed him.

Managing disappointment is a skill and a technique we need to learn and to practice in order to keep our own life under proper control, and to deal with those who disappoint us. Let us share some good ways to overcome disappointment.

1. Whatever happens to you, seek to maintain an even temperament with respect to both anger and sorrow.

2. Avoid becoming so emotional that you can't visualize the truths and complexities of a situation.

3. Maintain your own personal sense of fairness, no matter what the attitude of another may appear to be. Keep your best sense of perspective under control.

4. Remember that you may not be the only person experiencing disappointment. The person who has disappointed you may feel as badly as you, but not know how to share his or her feelings with you.

5. Disappointments rising out of misunderstood circumstances may turn out to be blessings in disguise, because they

afford an excuse to learn from each other, and arrive at the truth.

Let us always remember that when we trust in God, and leave the thread of life's design to his guidance, the pattern of life turns out much better than we expected. It is needful that we seek to be prayerful, forgiving, and ever willing to accept that which comes to pass as a result of love and trust in God, and in our fellow-beings.

Always keep your sense of humor. It helps to balance your feelings of disappointment. Someone has said, "It is a way of separating a temporary setback from the continuing joy of life."

We should never allow the pains of disappointment to cancel out friendships or close family ties. Sometimes disappointments serve in the end to make us closer than previously. You can allow your disappointments to help you become a "wounded healer." Henry Nouwen, a Roman Catholic priest, encourages us to let our wounds teach us in healing the wounds of others. Those of us who have experienced disappointments ought to try to become proficient in helping others with similar experiences, making better friends and alleviating our own anguish.

The Benediction:

May we go from this gathering, Lord, feeling better about ourselves and others than when we came. Grant that some of these thoughts may remain fresh in our minds, so that in the future, we won't be so easily hurt, or so judgmental in our reactions. Teach us how to live so as not to disappoint others or ourselves, and to recall the words of Paul: "Endurance produces character, and character produces hope, and hope does not disappoint us, because God's love has been poured into our hearts through the Holy Spirit that he has given to us." In Jesus' name. Amen.

26

The Full Measure
Of Life

Instrumental Meditation: "Wonderful Words Of Life"

A Brief Prayer: Psalm 39:4-5
> Lord, let me know my end, and what is the measure
> of my days; let me know how fleeting my life
> is.
> You have made my days a few handbreadths, and my
> lifetime is as nothing in thy sight.
> Surely everyone stands as a mere breath.

Hymn: "I'll Live For Him"

Scripture: Ephesians 4:11-15 (NRSV)
The gifts that he gave were that some would be apostles, some prophets, some evangelists, some pastors and teachers, to equip the saints for the work of ministry, for building up the body of Christ, until all of us come to the unity of the faith and of the knowledge of the Son of God, to maturity, to the measure of the full stature of Christ. We must no longer be children, tossed to and fro and blown about by every wind of doctrine, by people's trickery, by their craftiness in deceitful scheming. But speaking the truth in love, we must grow up in every way unto him who is the head, into Christ, from whom the whole body, joined and knit together by every ligament with which it is equipped, as each part is working properly, promotes the body's growth in building itself in love.

Another Prayer:

Gracious and loving God, we believe that you want us to enjoy the full measure of life, to be all that we can be, and to give as much of ourselves as we can for the sake of your kingdom on earth, as we look toward our life eternal. You have called us to serious and varied services, and have endowed us with talents and energy for fulfillment of our several callings. Enable us to come to the full stature of Christian maturity, spiritual stability, and the best use of the endowments you have bestowed upon us. We thank you for the gift of your Son, who has so nobly interpreted your Spirit, the way, the truth, and the life. Grant, O Lord, that we may live up to what we have found in him, who is our Lord and Savior. Amen.

Sermon: "The Full Measure Of Life"

A small envelope arrived in the mail, along with several larger ones. When it was opened, it read:

HELLO, WORLD!
My name is Jonathan James Taggart
I arrived at 9:01 p.m. Tuesday,
May 6, 1993
Weight: 8 lbs. 9 oz.
Length: 20 inches

It was the measure of a child who was to become a man; but there was no way to measure what the parents were feeling in their hearts. They had planned for the coming of a child, but there was no way to anticipate what the child was to become in the course of his lifetime. There was no way to know the measure of that new life.

Couples who have been happily married for many years experience the full measure of life together, but there is no way to adequately verbalize what they feel and know. They may only be able to say, "We love each other more now than at the beginning."

Many of us have been deeply committed Christians most of our lives. We know how we feel about our Lord and our beliefs, and that the assurance of our faith blesses and comforts us each day, and especially when the stresses, anxieties, and tragedies of life assail us. There is no way to give the accurate measurements of such a faith, but we know about its adequacy and sustenance for our lives, and we remember the words, "My grace is sufficient for you." (2 Corinthians 12:9)

Whatever our calling or vocation in life, we know that the great goal was well verbalized by Paul when he spoke about, "building up the body of Christ, until all of us come to the unity of faith and the knowledge of the Son of God, to maturity, to the measure of the full stature of Christ." It is so easy for us, as we become older in years, to stop growing intellectually and spiritually, imagining that we have arrived. That is a terrible fallacy, and we ought not to fall into its trap.

Life is not measured by calendar days only. It is also measured by the quality of life we live, by the degree of joy we offer and receive, and by the giving of ourselves, that we might know the true meaning of the life abundant.

When we begin to live primarily in the past, we are in danger of having a dim future. We can become so concerned with preserving what we've had, that we can't let go and gain what is needed now, which is a more vital relationship with the present. When we are afraid to change something in fear of losing everything we've been accustomed to, we stagnate, personally and spiritually. When people begin to live and act on the basis of fear rather than faith, we are in trouble. We must be willing to risk new visions for God and ourselves, else we will stop growing, and will lose the vitality of living creatively and joyously.

It is incumbent upon us in all stages of life, and urgently so for older persons, that we continue to grow in four areas: spiritual, physical, emotional, and intellectual. The full measure of life depends upon balance and reasonable strength in all of these categories.

The fullness of life! What a tremendous thought! It challenges us to be at our best, to be unafraid of the future, to more completely believe in God, and to believe in ourselves as his children, created in his divine image. We do well to remember the last phrases of the 23rd Psalm:

My cup runneth over.
Surely goodness and mercy shall follow me
all the days of my life:
and I will dwell in the house of the Lord
for ever. Amen.

Hymn: "Take My Life, And Let It Be"

The Benediction:
And now may the blessing of God Almighty, Father, Son and Holy Spirit, be among you and abide with you, now and evermore. Amen.

27

And Now, We Thank You, Our God

Meditation Music: "For All The Blessings Of The Year"
(May be effectively used as a vocal solo)

Words Of Preparation: Psalm 100:4-5
Enter his gates with thanksgiving, and his courts
with praise.
Give thanks to him, bless his name.
For the Lord is good: his steadfast love endures
forever, and his faithfulness to all generations.

Hymn: "Come, Ye Thankful People Come"

A Prayer Of Thanksgiving:
O our God, we praise you, and we give our heart-felt thanks
to you for all your bountiful providence, with all the blessings and all the hopes of life. Above all we praise and love
you for your unspeakable gift of your only Son our Lord and
Savior Jesus Christ. Let the memory of your goodness fill our
hearts with joy and thankfulness unto you, our Father, now
and evermore. Amen.

Scriptures: 1 Chronicles 29:10-13 (NRSV)
Then David blessed the Lord in the presence of all the as-
sembly; David said: "Blessed are you, O Lord, the God of
our ancestor Israel, forever and ever. Yours, O Lord are the

115

greatness, the power, the glory, the victory, and the majesty; for all that is in the heavens and on the earth is yours; yours is the kingdom, O Lord, and you are exalted as head above all. Riches and honor come from you, and you rule over all. In your hand are power and might; and it is in your hand to make great, and to give strength to all. And now, our God, we give thanks to you and praise your glorious name.''

Sermon: "And Now, We Thank You, Our God"

These words from 1 Chronicles 29:10-13 are some of the most powerful and impressive to be found in scripture. They are uplifting and magnificent. They were said by David to bless the Lord as the people came bringing their gifts to assure the building of a house for God. They are well worth our sincere thought as we come to the observance of Thanksgiving in this nation, in the spirit in which it was first done on December 4, 1619, and has been regularly done since it was proclaimed a national observance by President Lincoln in 1863.

We spend so much of our time thinking about what we want, and seeking help in attaining the stature of our desired being, that it is easy to overlook being seriously thankful. In the midst of the pressures of daily living and busy schedules, many people have abandoned the habit of saying grace before meals. Levels of noise, the mechanics of assemblage, the rush of getting things done, decimate the pause for spiritual assessment and expressing gratefulness.

We all need very much to recapture the awareness of the holy benevolence by which we are privileged to live and enjoy the provisions of Almighty God our Father. Many people do not regularly observe the preparation of food for meals, the making of clothing for our bodies, or the intricate processes of building shelters for our comfort and safety. Many people have not been on a farm where food is produced for many years, and have never witnessed this phenomena of growth and natural production, its harvest and preservation. Such unfamiliarity with the realities of life, conditions us to take life and its abundance for granted. Impersonal consumption adds to our loss of appreciation for our life and its sustenance.

People in nursing homes and hospitals seldom get a glimpse of cooks at work, or understand the detailed care by the dietitian and the food supervisor. To many, food is a choice made by selection from a printed menu. We do not get to select and handle the raw foods, and seldom enjoy the wonderful odors of a kitchen in preparation.

One day a grandmother and her seven-year-old grandson went to the food store together. He had not had opportunity to observe what goes on in a meat market. He was appalled by two halves of a lamb suspended on hooks. He saw a tub of hogs' heads, and remarked, "How gross!" When his grandmother purchased some beef, he asked, "Grandma, do they kill cows for that?" "Yes, they do," she replied, "and I have just gotten some beef to make the goulash that you like so much. It requires meat from cattle to make it good, the way you like it." For the first time he had a realistic introduction to the food chain, as he continued with her in the purchase of other food items.

Those of us who were fortunate enough to have lived on farms, grew turkeys, the corn for meal to make the dressing, executed and cleaned the bird, chopped wood for the stove, and made fire to heat the oven, may be much more aware of what this day means than are those who simply go to a cafeteria, and purchase prepared turkey and trimmings for the occasion. The age of automation and pre-preparation has robbed us of many of the details that add to the enjoyment and the excitement of what this day has traditionally meant.

True thanksgiving requires a keen awareness and consciousness of both bounty and sacrifice. David reminded those who brought gifts for the house of God of the divine resource that is ours to rejoice about, saying, "All things come from you, and of your own have we given you." (1 Chronicles 29:14) A choral sentence often used in connection with the offertory service, especially when there is a church choir, is, "All things

come of thee, O Lord, and of thine own have we given thee."
It is a reflection of David's words acknowledging our indebt-
edness to God for all he has given us. We should never allow
ourselves to forget this. Sacrificial love ought to be a part of
our thanksgiving. Loving enough to really care is essential to
being genuinely grateful.

We need to be careful in the midst of celebration and count-
ing our blessings, that we give thanks for the gift of God's
Son who became our Lord and Savior. We must not overlook
the praise of God in all our living, and especially at this time.
David declared, "Now we thank you our God, and praise your
glorious name." We should say or sing similar words today.

Hymn: "Now Thank We All Our God"

The Closing Prayer:
O Gracious God, on this day we have been blessed by your
Holy Presence in our midst. We thank you for families who
have blessed us with their love and remembrance as often as
possible, for friends, and all those who are special care-givers.
We thank you for helping and sustaining us in times of special need. Continue to abide in our hearts and lives, enriching
us with fond memories of worship and challenges for the living of our days, our years, and all our lives. In the name of
Jesus Christ our Lord. Amen.

28
There Is Wonderful News Today!

Meditation Music: "O Holy Night!"
(Would be excellent to set the scene as a solo)

The Story Of The Shepherds On The Night Of Jesus' Birth: from Luke 2:1-21 (TLB)

About this time Caesar Augustus, the Roman Emperor, decreed that a census should be taken throughout the nation. (This census was taken when Quirinius was governor of Syria.)

Everyone was required to return to his ancestral home for this registration. And because Joseph was a member of the royal line, he had to go to Bethlehem in Judea, King David's ancient home — journeying there from the Galilean village of Nazareth. He took with him Mary, his fiancée, who was obviously pregnant by this time.

And while they were there, the time came for her baby to be born; and she gave birth to her first child. She wrapped him in a blanket and laid him in a manger, because there was no room for them in the inn.

That night the shepherds were in the field outside the village, guarding their flocks of sheep. Suddenly an angel appeared among them, and the landscape shone with the glory of the Lord. They were badly frightened, but the angel reassured them.

"Don't be afraid," he said. "I bring you the most joyful news ever announced, and it is for everyone! The Savior —

yes, the Messiah, the Lord — has been born tonight in Bethlehem! How will you recognize him? You will find a baby wrapped in a blanket, lying in a manger.''

Suddenly the angel was joined by a vast host of others — the armies of heaven — praising God:

"Glory in the highest heaven," they sang, "and peace on earth for all those pleasing him.''

When the great army of angels had returned again to heaven the shepherds said to each other, "Come on! Let's go to Bethlehem! Let's see this wonderful thing that has happened, which the Lord has told us about.''

They ran to the village and found their way to Mary and Joseph. And there was the baby, lying in a manger. The shepherds told what had happened and what the angel had said to them about this child. All who heard the shepherd's story expressed astonishment, but Mary quietly treasured these things in her heart and often thought about them.

Then the shepherds went back again to their fields and flocks, praising God for the visit of the angels, and because they had seen the child, just as the angel had told them.

Hymn: "O Little Town Of Bethlehem"

A Christmas Prayer:

O God our Father, you have brought us again to the glad season when we celebrate the birth of your Son, Jesus Christ our Lord. Grant that his Spirit may be born anew in our hearts this day and that we may joyfully welcome him to reign over us. Open our ears that we may hear again the angelic chorus of old. Open our lips that we, too, may sing with uplifted hearts. "Glory to God in the highest, and on earth peace, good will toward all;'' through Jesus Christ our Lord. Amen.

Hymn: "Silent Night, Holy Night"

Sermon: "There Is Wonderful News Today"

The world is constantly in need of good news — news that will still our fears — news that will give us new hope and fresh understanding — news that is good instead of bad — news that will get our attention and hold it because it offers solutions for our life dilemmas.

The headline for that good news should be: "The Savior — yes, the Messiah — was born last night in Bethlehem!" and the sub-topic would be in the form of poetic praise: "Glory to God in the highest heaven, and peace on earth for all those pleasing him!" There were no televisions, newspapers, or radios, but the angelic army spread the good news, accompanied by a wonderful display of light and glory.

The impact was so strong that shepherds who heard the proclamation, responded with, "Come on! Let's go to Bethlehem! Let's see this wonderful thing that has happened."

There was good news! There was affirmation of it! There was enthusiastic response to it! Imagine what it would have been like if they had only had the communication tools we have today!

Do you recall the rejoicing that took place on May 8, 1945, when President Truman proclaimed victory in Europe, and again on August 14, 1945, when we celebrated V-J day? Church bells rang, there was joy in the streets, people gathered in churches to offer prayers of thanksgiving to God that peace was again coming after long and sorrowful struggles. The promise of peace was something to rejoice the hearts of all of us! Unfortunately, the Vietnam conflagration did not end in the same fashion. Nevertheless peace on earth, good will among men continues to be our sincere desire and goal.

According to The Living Bible, the good news was for everyone! And that is still wonderful news for us today. Jesus Christ was born in history at just the right time to get the world's attention in a most memorable way. He came to teach, preach, and give himself in such a way that people were convinced that he was truly the Son of God and the Savior of the world. He offered salvation for every person and people of the world.

121

The good news did not conclude with exaltations at the feet of the child born in a manger. The Christmas message did not conclude with the arrival of the Wise Men, at the cross, in the grave or with the resurrection; rather it goes on after all these events, for it is the good news of salvation for all who will accept it.

Again, as on that first Christmas, there is wonderful news for everyone today. Let us accept it in our hearts, and share it with all whom we meet. May the joys of Christmas and the good news of our Lord abide with each and all, now and evermore. "Don't be afraid!" the angel said, "I bring you the most wonderful news ever announced, and it is for everyone!"

Hymns: "Joy To The World, The Lord Is Come!" and "O Come, Let Us Adore Him"

The Postlude: "Silent Night, Holy Night!"

29

He Has Come Back To Life!

Instrumental Meditation

Words Of Preparation *(By the Worship Leader)*
Blessed be the God and Father of our Lord Jesus Christ!
By his great mercy we have been born anew to a living hope
through the resurrection of Jesus Christ from the dead.

Hallelujah! For the Lord our God the Almighty reigns. The
kingdom of the world has become the kingdom of our Lord
and of his Christ, and he shall reign for ever and ever, King
of kings and Lord of lords. Hallelujah!

Thanks be to God who gives us the victory!

Let us sing with great rejoicing!

Hymn: "Christ The Lord Is Risen Today!"

An Invocation:
O loving God, who through your only Son has overcome
death, and opened unto us the gate of everlasting life, grant
we humbly ask you, that we who celebrate our Lord's resurrection, may, by the renewing of your Spirit, rise from the
death of sin to the life of righteousness; through Jesus Christ,
our Lord and Savior. Amen.

Part Of The Easter Story: Mark 16:1-8 (NRSV)
When the Sabbath was over, Mary Magdalene, and Mary
the mother of James and Salome, brought spices so that they

might go and anoint him. And very early on the first day of the week when the sun had risen, they went to the tomb. They had been saying to one another, "Who will roll away the stone for us from the entrance to the tomb?" When they looked up, they saw that the stone, which was very large, had already been rolled back. As they entered the tomb, they saw a young man, dressed in a white robe, sitting on the right side, and they were alarmed. But he said to them, "Do not be alarmed; you are looking for Jesus of Nazareth, who was crucified. He has been raised; he is not here. Look, there is the place they laid him. But go, tell his disciples and Peter that he is going ahead of you to Galilee; there you will see him just as he told you. So they went out and fled from the tomb, for terror and amazement had seized them; and they said nothing to anyone, for they were afraid.

Hymn: "Christ Arose"

Sermon: "He Has Come Back To Life"

The Living Bible Paraphrased makes Mark 16:6 sound like the language we speak. Listen.

The angel said, "Don't be surprised. Aren't you looking for Jesus, the Nazarene who was crucified? He isn't here! He has come back to life! Look, that's where his body was lying."

He has risen! He has come back to life! He isn't here!

It would have been incomprehensible to everyone had they not known that Lazarus had been brought back to life on the initiative of Jesus. But Lazarus had not suffered in the manner that Jesus did. How could this be?

The 20th chapter of John tells us that early on Sunday morning the first person to see him alive again was Mary Magdalene, and that she went to the disciples and told them that she had seen Jesus, and he was alive! They found it hard to believe what she told them, because the disciples had forgotten what he said when he had cleansed the temple. Memory

tends to falter when we are traumatized and confused by tragedy and grief.

Jesus came back to life because he promised he would. He
returned to the living state to assure us that there is life beyond the experience we call death. He was living proof that
immortality is a reality, not a figment of the imagination or
idealistic dreaming, but a truth well demonstrated.

He came back to life to re-establish confidence in the meaning of life itself. He made real the truth of the scriptures as
he traveled along the Emmaus road, and he broke bread with
some men at a table, so that they recognized him by the nail
prints in his hands. Those men rushed back to Jerusalem to
tell others, who were still reluctant to accept their story, until
Jesus appeared in that room with them, even as they discussed
what they were hearing.

Jesus came back to life to do away with doubt concerning
who he was. A week after Easter he came back to that same
place, and Thomas, who still had reservations, was with them
this time. Jesus invited Thomas, because he wanted tangible
proof, to examine his wounds, and when he looked closely,
Thomas exclaimed, "My Lord and my God!"

Jesus came back to life to re-establish love in the Christian sense, and to renew the comprehension of Christian
responsibility. He preferred that they make enemies into
friends, and win their souls for God's kingdom.

When the disciples were confused and unsure about how
to proceed, Jesus met them at the seashore, giving them courage
for their personal tasks, and to renew the fellowship for their
nurture, providing them with counsel and encouragement. He
talked with them about the main task of their lives — the care
and nurture of God's flock — in an on-going ministry. If they
really loved him, they would devote their lives to what he had
begun.

And Jesus returned to life to impart a sense of divine commission in which all people might share. He said to them, "All
authority in heaven and on earth has been given to me. Go
therefore and make disciples of all nations, baptizing them

in the name of the Father, and of the Son, and of the Holy Spirit, and teaching them to obey everything that I have commanded you. And remember, I am with you always, to the end of the age."

It is true: Jesus came back to fulfill his promise, to assure us that there is life beyond death, to do away with doubt about his identity and purpose, to re-establish the meaning of Christian love and its accompanying responsibilities, and to include all of us in the divine commission. He came back to life to allay our fears and to impart courage and authority for abundant life and divine sharing.

Hymn: "He Lives!"

The Sending Forth:

Go now in the power of life that was discovered on the day of Jesus' resurrection, knowing that death is not final, but only the opening of the door to life eternal. Live at your best, rejoice in spiritual triumphs, and serve God through Christ, knowing that what he taught as the way, the truth, and the life will make our life abundant beyond our imagination. Go then in peace and in power. Amen.

An Appropriate Instrumental Postlude: *(Perhaps Handel's "Hallelujah Chorus")*

30
Like A New Batch Of Dough

Meditation Music Appropriate To Observance Of The Eucharist

Words Of Preparation:
Behold, I stand at the door and knock; if anyone hears my voice and opens the door, I will come in and eat with him, and he with me. (Revelation 3:20)

The cup which we bless, is it not a participation in the blood of Christ? The bread which we break, is it not a participation in the body of Christ? (1 Corinthians 10:16)

A Prayer:
Almighty God, unto whom all hearts are open, all desires known, and from whom no secrets are hidden: Cleanse the thoughts of our hearts by the inspiration of your Holy Spirit, that we may perfectly love you, and worthily magnify your holy name; through Jesus Christ our Lord. Amen.

The Lord's Prayer

Scripture: 1 Corinthians 5:6b-8 (NRSV)
Do you not know that a little yeast leavens the whole batch of dough? Clean out the old yeast so that you may be a new batch, as you really are unleavened. For our paschal lamb, Christ, has been sacrificed. Therefore let us celebrate the

127

festival, not with the old yeast, the yeast of malice and evil, but with the unleavened bread of sincerity and truth.

Hymn: "Break Thou The Bread Of Life"

The Sermon: "Like A New Batch Of Dough"
*(In preparation of observance
of the Sacrament of Holy Communion)*

We do well to remember that Paul had grown up in the faith of strict Judaism, and had become a very knowledgeable person in matters of Jewish law and ritual. The goodness of those strict observances had stuck with him as they applied to Christian motives and conduct. He was very conscious of the relationship between the Jewish Passover and the Christian observance of the Lord's supper.

Paul's purpose in writing to the Corinthians was to clarify the idea of what it means to be a Christian, and to conscientiously live the Christian life. He had been perturbed by some of the things he was hearing about them, and wanted them to get rid of the sins about which he had learned, and to motivate the people of his ministry to be pure in the whole of their lives.

The sanctified life is not easy, but it is desirable, and the observance of the Sacrament should help in sustaining it. Righteousness in every circumstance of our being is most needful. There is no such thing as being a little bit sinful, and Paul reminds us that "a little yeast leavens the whole batch of dough."

The Jewish custom demanded that every scrap of the old yeast, including the crumbs from leavened bread, should be removed from the house before sharing the Passover, which included unleavened bread. We, as Christians need to get rid of the least trace of sin in the same manner. To rid ourselves of the leaven of sins, self-examination is necessary; so is self-discipline. Knowing about a matter is not enough; we must do something about it! We do not do this entirely by our own power alone. By the grace of God through his Son Jesus Christ this is made possible.

Our purpose should not be just to get by with the minimum religious duties, but to have as our goal, "Be perfect, therefore, as your heavenly Father is perfect." (Matthew 5:48) In matters of faith and salvation we must never do less than our best. The Good News Bible reads, "You must remove the old yeast of sin so that you will be entirely pure. Then you will be like a new batch of dough without any yeast." (1 Corinthians 5:7)

Forms and rituals are not of themselves sufficient religious processes. Sincerity and change must come from within, and must abide as conscious effect in our lives and behavioral manifestations. Sermons may be of assistance, but to be fully helpful they must be gospel truth applied to life. We must not just hear and say, "That is true." We should also put the truth into action. We must receive and be nurtured by the bread of truth.

We come here to celebrate a sacred religious observance, determined to get rid of the old yeast of sin, and to begin again with new dough, that we might receive the bread of purity and truth.

Let us heed the counsel of Paul as found in 1 Corinthians 11:27-29: "Whoever eats the bread or drinks the cup in an unworthy manner will be answerable for the body and the blood of the Lord. Examine yourselves, and only then eat the bread and drink of the cup. For all who eat and drink without discerning the body, eat and drink judgment against themselves."

Hymn: "Jesus Spreads His Banner O'er Us"

The Observance Of The Eucharist: *(Conducted by an ordained minister, or properly authorized person, in keeping with the Christian faith and ecumenical customs, using the preferred ritual of choice.)*

The Parting Hymn: "God Be With You"

The Instrumental Postlude

129

An Index Of
Scripture References

www.ingramcontent.com/pod-product-compliance
Lightning Source LLC
LaVergne TN
LVHW021513080426
835509LV00018B/2498